£11.95

D0281627

MOORE'S INTRODUCTION TO
ENGLISH
CANON LAW

MOORE'S INTRODUCTION TO
ENGLISH
CANON LAW

Second Edition

BY

E. GARTH MOORE

*Chancellor of the Dioceses of Durham, Southwark
and Gloucester
Fellow of Corpus Christi College, Cambridge
Clerk in Holy Orders
Of Gray's Inn, Barrister-at-Law
and*

TIMOTHY BRIDEN

*of the Inner Temple,
Barrister-at-Law*

MOWBRAY
LONDON & OXFORD

ISBN 0 264 66901 0 (hardback)
ISBN 0 264 66854 5 (paperback)
First published 1967 by the Clarendon Press

This revised edition published 1985
by A. R. Mowbray & Co. Ltd,
Saint Thomas House, Becket Street,
Oxford, OX1 1SJ

British Library Cataloguing in Publication Data

Moore, E. Garth
    Moore's introduction to English canon law.—
    2nd rev. ed.
    1. Church of England   2. Canon law
    I. Title   II. Briden, Timothy
    262.9   KD8642

    ISBN 0-264-66901-0 (hardback)
    ISBN 0-264-66854-5 (paperback)

Printed in Great Britain by
Biddles Ltd., Guildford.

PREFACE
to First Edition

IN writing a short book about a large subject the difficulty is to know what to omit. This book is full of omissions. What has been attempted is twofold; first, to present the elements, which involves dealing, however inadequately, with profundities (for something which is truly elementary is profound and seldom easy); and, secondly, to give an outline, and only an outline, of what has developed from these elements. If a practising lawyer unacquainted with ecclesiastical law is suddenly presented with a problem within a narrow scope, he is at a serious disadvantage by reason of his ignorance of the background against which his problem is set. He soon finds that he cannot see the wood for the trees. For him a book such as this may be a help. It probably will not answer his immediate problem; but it may enable him, with the use of more detailed works, to approach his problem from the proper angle. It is partly for him that this book is intended. It is also intended for the ordinand and for the ordained man, who are all too often given no instruction whatever in a subject which touches their rights, their obligations and their theology at every point. In this respect the Church compares most unfavourably with the secular professions in which an outline knowledge of the law immediately affecting the practitioner and those whom he serves is usually a condition precedent to practice. It may, too, be a help to members of the Church Assembly and others who are interested in canon law revision. To revise something about which one knows nothing is a difficult and dangerous exercise.

It is with these considerations in mind that this book has been written. References have been reduced to a minimum and many details have been omitted. No one with a concrete problem can safely rely on this book alone to provide the answer. But it may help him to understand the answer, when he gets it from another source, and it may help him to find that source.

I have tried as far as possible to present controversial matters factually and impartially. If, as is probable, I have not always succeeded, I hope that it is at least clear when I am expressing an opinion and not stating a fact. If it be thought that a great deal of emphasis has been placed on the Establishment, it must be remembered that this is a book about English canon law and that in England the Establishment is an important factor. It is hoped that this emphasis has not tended to obscure the even more important fact that the Church's authority, though expressed through many human agencies, claims to be derived from Christ himself. When the law is bad, it is human fallibility which is the cause, and the fault sometimes lies in the nature of the legislative, executive, or judicial machinery; and in canon law revision, though details may be important and require revision, the fundamental task of the reformer is to remedy the defects in the human machinery so that God's will may perfectly be reflected in his Church's laws.

The law is as stated on the 1 September 1965; but in some of the footnotes reference is made to subsequent or proposed legislation.

E. GARTH MOORE

Corpus Christi College
Cambridge

PREFACE

to Second Edition

THE first edition of this book, while still, it is hoped, basically adequate, is in many minor respects now out of date. Indeed, such is the volume of modern legislation, that even this edition will have been overtaken by it before publication. Certainly the Church of England has had much about which to legislate. For over three centuries there had been virtually no new Canons, and those of 1603–4 were hopelessly inadequate to meet modern requirements, while, in the field of major legislation, until the Enabling Act, 1919, only Parliament could legislate, with the result that not very much of outstanding importance had occurred since the Act of Uniformity, 1662. The former Church Assembly and its successor, General Synod, can, therefore, offer a credible *apologia* for much of their legislative activities in the field of administrative reform.

But, though General Synod is the successor to Church Assembly, its powers are wider, in that it can in some matters legislate by Canon, which, though requiring the Royal Assent, does not need Parliamentary approval. There is now, therefore, in practical terms, a larger measure of autonomy, especially in the field of liturgical reform. Since doctrine is inextricably bound up with liturgy, as sometimes is discipline, this has meant that matters of theology have played a larger part in the deliberations of General Synod, despite the fact that it is not the ideal forum for theological discussion. Traditionally the bishops are the custodians of doctrine, and formerly doctrinal matters were raised in Convocation where the bishops had the advantage of hearing the views of the Clergy in Convocation, among whom was always a number of theologians. The bishops were thus better placed, if legislation was required, to present the House of Laity with a scheme for approval which had already undergone some degree of theological consideration. This was strictly in accordance with the canonical tradition that the bishops are the prime custodians of the Faith, advised by the clergy, but ultimately putting their deliberations to the laity in order to receive the *consensus fidelium*.

Perhaps the time has come to remember that, though Convocation is not a legislative forum, its deliberations are by no means obsolete or useless and that both Convocations should now be encouraged to meet more often to discuss theological implications in depth before Measures involving doctrine are presented to General Synod. Such a course might obviate the inconclusive deliberations in General Synod which we have witnessed over the questions of marriage and divorce. For anything concrete to have emerged from those debates legislation would have been required, and, therefore, the consent of the House of Laity. But such legislation, to be sound, must be based on sound doctrine, and this requires a degree of expertise more likely to be found after discussion in depth in Convocation.

In presenting this second edition to the public, we therefore venture to suggest that, not only will the bishops be better placed to exercise their traditional role, but also that the legislative functions of General Synod will in future be facilitated and the volume of its work reduced if, in matters involving doctrine, preliminary consideration is given by both Houses of Convocation, whether sitting separately or together.

London, 1985   E. GARTH MOORE
                                                  TIMOTHY BRIDEN

CONTENTS

TABLE OF STATUTES

TABLE OF MEASURES

TABLE OF CANONS

TABLE OF CASES

I

INTRODUCTION

'IN the beginning God created the heaven and the earth.' There, in the opening words of Genesis, is the root of our study of the canon law. In the study of moral theology we are concerned with the whole of God's law in so far as it is immediately relevant to man. In the study of the canon law we are concerned with so much of the moral law as is enforced, directly or indirectly, by human sanctions. The basis of the canon law is theological. When the atheist objects that, since there is no God, there can be no divine law, he is attacking the root concept upon which the canon law is based and the Christian must meet him on the field of theology. If the lawyer objects, as some do, that the divine law cannot be ascertained, the reply is again a theological one, for the Christian claims that there is a God, that God has a will, that in many instances that will has been revealed, and that, for the Christian, God's revealed will is law. The Christian goes on further to say that, whether or not this theological foundation is acceptable to the lawyer, the lawyer must at least concede that, in the human field, canon law is real law inasmuch as it is enforced by sanctions. The lawyer need often look no further. He need not normally concern himself with whether the theological root of the canon law is sound or unsound. It is usually enough for him to know what is and what is not enforced by human agents. But, if he satisfies himself with this superficial approach, he will sooner or later run into difficulties, for the interpretation and administration of the law cannot be satisfactorily conducted without an understanding of what lies behind it. The canonist, therefore, can never be simply a lawyer; he must always be in some measure a theologian, and he will frequently require the assistance of historians.

His study begins with the first verse of the first chapter of Genesis, and the whole of Scripture is directly or indirectly concerned with it. 'In the beginning God created the heaven and the earth'; and, if with the Almighty creation and legislation are the same thing, that is the first recorded piece of divine legislation.

Indeed, the language of legislation is employed throughout the creation story; 'God said, let there be light: and there was light.' But, even if it be insisted that there is distinction between legislation and creation, one does not have to read further than the twenty-eighth verse of the first chapter to find God's first direct command to Man: 'Be fruitful and multiply and replenish the earth and subdue it.' The first direct prohibition is in the second chapter; 'Of the tree of the knowledge of good and evil, thou shalt not eat.' So throughout the Old Testament God's law is revealed, often implicitly, sometimes explicitly, as in the giving of the Ten Commandments to Moses; and in the New Testament our Lord in His summary gives the twofold substance of that law, both implicit and explicit, as love towards God and love towards one's neighbour, upon which hang all the law and the prophets.

But (for the immediate matter in hand more important still) our Lord both implicitly and explicitly delegated His law-making authority to what today we should call a subordinate legislature, when He bestowed the power of the keys and the power to bind and to loose upon His Church, the Body which He left behind on earth, there to carry on His work, which in its amplitude embraces, among much else, the functions of the law-maker who gives the law and of the judge who, as well as exonerating and condemning, interprets. It is at this point that canon law, though stemming from general theology, begins to be recognizable as a distinct subject in its own right.

The legislative (and judicial) authority of the Church has been exercised in different ways at different times and places and has, like much else, grown from a small seed into a mighty tree. But it has two important characteristics. The first is that it does not stand alone; it is the inheritor of the whole law of God in so far as that is at any moment relevant. The second is that, like all subordinate legislative authority, it has validity only within the framework of its principal and parent, the divine law. Thus it is within the competence of the Church to make and adopt rules concerning the incidentals of marriage[1] and to vary them from time to time and from place to place. It can, for

---

[1.]   See Chapter IX *post*.

example, insist that a marriage shall take place only in church after publication of banns; or it can, on the other hand, permit and recognize the validity of a purely secular ceremony before the temporal authority. But is is *ultra vires* the Church to vary the nature of marriage, for that is already determined by the divine law with the framework of which alone the Church's delegated authority can operate. If then, the divine law ordains that a marriage is the union of one man with one woman for life, it does not lie within the competence of the Church to permit the second marriage of divorced persons whose first partners are still living, for that would be an impossibility as contrary to the creative-legislative ordinance of God regarding the essential nature of marriage.[2] Wide, then, as is the scope of the Church's legislative authority, it is, nevertheless, a limited authority.

It is impossible in a short space to trace in more than the barest outline the gradual development of the canon law. In the early Church local custom, varied or controlled by local episcopal regulation, soon built up a series of elastic and rudimentary systems. Later, local councils and General Councils issued canons of more general application and, with the growth of papal authority, the decretals of popes assumed an ever-growing importance. These papal decretals had about them something of the nature of case-law, for they were answers to specific questions put to Rome by inferior authorities. It was inevitable that in course of time industrious clerks should set about collecting and arranging these scattered and diverse pronouncements, and thus codes came into existence. Their authors were not always above forging a decretal, if they were short of the genuine material, though be it said that, just as a decretal might be declaratory of existing law as well as the author of new law, so these forged decretals were probably perfectly sound expositions of the law and won acceptance as such.

The subjects covered by this body of law were very varied and included matters of theology, liturgics, discipline in the widest

---

[2.] This undoubtedly was the Western Catholic and Anglican position for centuries. In June 1983 the General Synod passed a resolution, not yet (1984) enacted in legislative form, to the effect that in certain circumstances a divorced person might be 'remarried' in church. If this resolution should be implemented, it will mark a change in the doctrine of the Church of England.

sense, and the ordering of all aspects of Church life.

England, like the rest of Western Christendom, was caught up in this general growth of the canon law, and, like the rest of Western Christendom, it had its own local complications. These might be no more than the normal variations introduced by provincial or diocesan regulations (though consistent with the general law of the Church), or they might be the more serious complications which resulted from royal legislation in fields where king and pope both sought supremacy. Thus, for example, in England the temporal courts succeeded in gaining effective control over advowsons[3] while all sorts of matters, such as defamation, which we should regard as primarily secular, were recognized as within the province of the ecclesiastical tribunals. So long as king and pope indulged in intermittent warfare or uneasy truce, it was necessary for lawyers to know something both of the common law and of the canon law, if they were adequately to do their work. Indeed, the same man might well be eminent in both fields, with what ultimate effect upon the development both of the common law and of the canon law it is difficult to assess.

When Henry VIII ascended the throne there were in existence two complete systems of courts, the spiritual and the temporal; and, since the Church was established (in that it did not occur to anyone that there could be a hard and fast line between Church and State), the spiritual courts could for practical purposes be said to be as much a part of the State as were the king's courts, and their judgements were as effectively enforced. They were, however, in many respects very different from each other, both in the law which they administered and in their procedure. The Church's law, being common to so many countries which had once acknowledged the sway of Imperial Rome and now owed a common allegiance to the Roman pontiff, drew heavily upon the Roman civil law for the training of its lawyers and for its practice and for its jurisprudential concepts and for its language. For its substantive[4] law,

---

[3.] The right to present to a living.

[4.] Evidence and procedure are called *adjectival law* because they exist to facilitate the enforcement of the *substantive law* which is concerned with what may or may not be. The substantive law prohibits and defines murder. Adjectival law directs how a murder trial shall be conducted.

however, it looked to the general codes and canons and decretals and to the ordinances of the provinces of Canterbury and York and of the local diocese, and, of course, to the Church's concept of the basic law of God, yet always, of necessity, with a sidelong glance (reluctant or relieved) at royal legislation.

Then came the Reformation, which had as its immediate object and effect the termination of the papal authority within this realm and the declaration that the king should be accepted and reputed the only supreme head on earth of the Church of England. But that, of course, was only the beginning, and soon Faith as well as Order was involved in a cauldron which was to bubble vigorously for many years before subsiding into the state of chronic, if gentle, simmering to which we have grown accustomed. The operation of cutting loose from the papal authority severed this country from a legislative source of very great importance; henceforth changes in the law of the Church of England could come only by or with the express or implied consent of the secular power. This was soon to mean that for the papal supremacy we had substituted a parliamentary supremacy; for the ecclesiastical cauldron was not the only pot on the fire, and the next 150 years was to see the shifting of power from the king in person to the King in Parliament.

But though no new canon law would come from Rome, the whole body of the canon law which had already accumulated and been accepted in this country still remained in so far as it was not inconsistent with the Reformation settlement. Ecclesiastical courts continued to flourish, and ecclesiastical lawyers showed themselves as well versed as their predecessors in the system of jurisprudence which had been built up before the Reformation. Their task, however, was now more complicated; for, in addition to having to decide as need arose how far the pre-Reformation law had been abrogated, they also, and in growing measure, had to pay direct regard to Acts of Parliament which henceforth were to be their undisputed source of all changes in the law.

But even in the sixteenth and seventeeth centuries, despite the intense and general interest in matters theological, the secular power sometimes had the wisdom to see that the minutiae at least of ecclesiastical legislation were better left to more expert, though subordinate, legislatures. Fortunately these legislatures were to hand in the form of the ancient Convocations of Canterbury and York, each consisting of an Upper House of bishops and (unlike the usual continental provincial synod) of a Lower House of representatives, elected and *ex officio*, of the inferior clergy. The precise limits to the powers of these two bodies, both probably older than Parliament, had never been determined in pre-Reformation times. After the Reformation they were recognized as having power to make canons, which, however, like Acts of Parliament, required the royal assent before acquiring any validity. Even so, their effect was limited. They were of no effect whatever if contrary to the general law of the land, whether statutory or common law; and they were of themselves binding on no one except ecclesiastical *personae*, that is, in the main, the clergy and a few others such as churchwardens and chancellors. The result in effect was that the Sovereign in Convocation could make by-laws for the governance of the clergy of either province, provided that these did not run contrary to the general law of the land.

Various attempts at legislation along these limited lines were made by the Convocations during the formative years of the Reformation in the sixteenth century; but they came to nothing until in the reign of James I that body of law known as the Canons of 1603 (or 1604) was passed by the Convocations of both provinces and received the royal assent. They cover a variety of subjects, some trivial and some important; but they form only a very small portion indeed of the whole field of canon law. A good deal of what they say is merely declaratory or repetitive of selected bits of the general law of the Church; some canons were simply repetitions of pre-Reformation canons; some give directions regarding the dress of the clergy, both in and out of church (and even in their beds, or at least in their houses);[5] and the whole is a hotch-potch of the matters, big and small, which at the beginning of the seventeenth century it was thought desirable to produce or reproduce for the clergy in some sort of legislative form. Even a historian expert in that period might be hard put to it to explain fully why some matters were included and some omitted from this curious body of canons. Of them the late Bishop Hensley Henson wrote:

[5] Canon 74 of 1603.

Let any candid and loyal clergyman be at the pains of reading through the Canons of 1604 (which form the bulk of our canonical code) and let him consider how he could reasonably and usefully make them his rule of action. He will certainly rise from his study with a feeling of dismay, so remote are they from the circumstances of his life, so harsh their tone, so frankly impracticable are many of their practical requirements.[6]

The Bishop's condemnation has been generally endorsed, and has found practical expression in the energy expended in the twentieth century in seeking to revise these canons—a process which has proved difficult and tedious in that they form part of the Reformation settlement, a nicely balanced and at times precarious structure reflecting great credit on its seventeenth-century architects, who had to display all the genius of tightrope walkers. On one side lay the decadent abuses of unreformed Rome; on the other the excesses of the grosser forms of nonconformity. Catholic truths had to be preserved and restated in terms which were acceptable to Protestant zeal. The future could not be jeopardized by the surrender of essentials; and yet the immediate and crying need was peace. The resilience which for more than two centuries that settlement has displayed is a remarkable tribute to its authors' work. It is not, however, surprising that what was designed very largely with an eye to the needs of the seventeenth century should, by the twentieth century, appear in places a little threadbare and ill-fitting.

The process of revising the canons came to fruition in 1964, with the promulgation of fresh canons which, together with those of 1969, were intended substantially to replace the canons of 1603. A further important change occurred in 1970, with the transfer to the General Synod of the Church of England of the powers of the Convocations to legislate by canon.[7] The Convocations now have no residual powers to make canons. Since 1970, the Canons of 1964 and 1969 have been expanded and modified by the General Synod, a legislative process which seems likely to continue indefinitely.

Though for a long period the Canons of 1603 remained substantially unchanged, though for a century and a half the Convocations did nothing but formal business, though Rome

---

6. Retrospect of an Unimportant Life, vol. i, p.299.
7. Synodical Government Measure 1969 (No.2) S.1 and Schedule 1; Canon H1.

no longer ruled, there remained instead the Royal Supremacy, transformed into a parliamentary supremacy, and Acts of Parliament became the recognized normal mode of altering the law of the Church as well as the law of the State. Among these, of outstanding importance is the Act of Uniformity, 1662,[8] which has as its schedule the Book of Common Prayer, wherein is enshrined much of the theology of the Church of England. If one wishes to discover the doctrine of any Church, one should look early at the formularies by which it regulates its worship, and the Church of England is no exception. The Book of Common Prayer is, of course, the work of churchmen,[9] and of churchmen who were conscious of the delicacy of their task in giving expression to the teaching of a Church at once Catholic and Reformed. The language which they employed had, as far as possible, to satisfy many conflicting factions so as to embrace within one fold as many Englishmen as possible without sacrificing truth, for the Church claimed to be at once both the Church of the English and a part of the Catholic Church of Christ. But, though the Prayer Book is the work of churchmen, its legal authority is derived from Parliament, and its embodiment in the Act of Uniformity is the nation's acceptance of it. But for over three centuries Parliament was concerned also with matters less basic to the life of the Church than the Act of Uniformity. All the Church's legislation, great and small, was done by Act of Parliament. By the twentieth century, with the increase of all legislation, parliamentary time was more and more difficult to spare, and Members of Parliament were no longer uniformly Anglican. Meanwhile the Church had set up the Church Assembly, and in 1919 Parliament passed the 'Enabling Act'[10] which bestowed upon the Church Assembly (in 1970 renamed and reconstituted as the General Synod)[11] the right to pass Measures having the full force of Acts of Parliament. These Measures require the royal assent, which cannot be given until both Houses of Parliament have agreed to their submission. Thus parliamentary supremacy remains a reality; but in practice the day-to-day legislation of the Church is initiated and carried through by the Church itself. Parliament,

---

[8]   14 Car. II, c.4.
[9]   This should be remembered when interpreting its rubrics: see p.54. post (No.2).
[10] Church of England Assembly (Powers) Act, 1919 (9 & 10 Geo. V, c.76).
[11] Synodical Government Measure 1969 (No.2) s.2.

of course, has not surrendered its legal right to legislate directly
for the Church, and conflict between the General Synod and
Parliament or between the General Synod and the Ministers of
the Crown is always possible and has occurred, notably in the
rejection by Parliament of the Revised Prayer Books put
forward by its predecessor the Church Assembly in proposed
Measures in 1927 and 1928. In the event of unresolved conflict,
it is the will of Parliament or of the Crown which, for good or ill,
in law prevails. But assuming, as is normally the case, that a
proposed Measure of the General Synod receives the royal
assent, it becomes part of the law of the land.

In the light of this brief survey it would now be as well to
summarize the situation.

Canon law has its roots in theology. But, so far as England
is concerned, it may be defined as so much of the law of
England as is concerned with the regulation of the affairs of
the Church of England.

Its sources may be conveniently summarized as follows:

1. Theology, to be culled from the usual theological sources,
   first and foremost from the Bible, but also from many other
   sources of various weight, such as the patristic writings, the
   opinions of other authors, the pronouncements of
   Lambeth Conferences, liturgical formularies, the views of
   the Convocations, and much else besides. This is a flexible
   and imprecise list; but theology, though the queen of the
   sciences, is not itself a precise science. All that is here
   indicated is that, in order to ascertain the law of the
   Church, it is at times necessary to return to first principles,
   and that the main structure of the canon law is based on the
   (often hidden) foundations of theology.

2. The whole body of pre-Reformation canon law, in so far as
   this has not been altered by or since the Reformation.
   Much of this, like the common law of England, has never
   been authoritatively written. Much of it appears in
   rescripts, decretals, and old canons, the real value of which
   lies in the light which they throw upon what was commonly
   accepted by the Church.

3. The common law of England, that is, in this context, the
   unwritten law of the English, to be culled in the main from
   the reports of decided cases.

4. Acts of Parliament.

5. Measures of Church Assembly and the General Synod.
6. The canons of the two Convocations and the General Synod.
7. The subordinate legislation of persons and bodies acting in pursuance of an authority properly delegated by law. This includes a wide variety of legislative acts, such as Orders in Council made by the Queen under the authority of an Act of Parliament or a Measure, Statutory Rules and Orders, the by-laws of local government authorities, and much else besides.

II

THE CONSTITUTION: (I) THE ESTABLISHMENT

Being by God's Ordinance, according to Our just Title, Defender of the Faith and Supreme Governor of the Church, within these Our Dominions, We hold it most agreeable to this Our Kingly Office, and Our own religious zeal, to conserve and maintain the Church committed to Our Charge, in Unity of true Religion, and in the Bond of Peace. . . . We have therefore, upon mature Deliberation, and with the Advice of so many of Our Bishops as might conveniently be called together, thought fit to make this Declaration following. . . . That We are Supreme Governor of the Church of England. . . .

So runs the Royal Declaration which is the Preface to the Thirty-nine Articles of the Church of England, and it leaves the reader in no doubt concerning the position in the Church claimed by the Sovereign. It is, however, to be noted that the claim is limited to 'the Church within these our Dominions'. This is emphasized again in Article XXXVII, where it is further made clear that the claim is limited to the right to *rule*.

The King's Majesty hath the chief power in this Realm of England, and other his Dominions, unto whom the chief Government of all Estates of this Realm, whether they be Ecclesiastical or Civil, in all causes doth appertain, and is not, nor ought to be, subject to any foreign jurisdiction. . . . We give not to our Princes the ministering either of God's Word, or of the Sacraments . . . but that only prerogative, which we see to have been given always to all Godly Princes in holy Scriptures by God himself; that is, that they should rule all estates and degrees committed to their charge by God, whether they be Ecclesiastical or Temporal, and restrain with the civil sword the stubborn and evildoers.

Then comes the significant sentence which reveals what was really weighing on the minds of Englishmen during the formative years of the Reformation: 'The Bishop of *Rome* hath no jurisdiction in this Realm of *England*.' The royal claims were being emphasized as a counterblast to the papal claims. The sovereign independence of the English in matters secular was imperilled by its denial in matters spiritual, and the champion and symbol of independence in both spheres was the king.

If we were treating of the whole Catholic Church, this is not the point at which we should begin the constitutional section of the work. But we are primarily concerned with a part only of the Catholic Church, namely, that part which is by law established within this realm of England. It is, therefore, probably more convenient to begin with an examination of the nature of the Establishment which forms, as it were, the framework within which the picture itself is set; and we must admit at the outset that, while the Establishment may be easy to recognize, it is difficult to describe and more difficult still to define. Since, however, the Church of England is in law 'regarded as the branch of the Church which was founded in England when the English were gradually converted to Christianity between the years 597 and 687',[1] some attempt must be made to understand at least the implications of the Establishment. In order to understand the nature of establishment it is perhaps best to look first at two extremes, and for these it is necessary to go abroad.

At one end of the scale, in the United States of America there is no established religion. Various persons choose to associate together for a variety of purposes. Some do so in clubs for purely social purposes; others do so in order to further their common political views; yet others do so for the purpose of common worship, and these associations are often called Churches. But in law they are simply the free association of persons who contractually agree to be bound by certain common rules, and, provided their purpose and means of achieving it are not unlawful, the law is seldom concerned with what these are and seldom has occasion to differentiate between, for example, an association for the promotion of music and an association for the promotion of some religious object.

The other extreme is to be found in ancient Jewry. There the identification of what we should call Church and State was complete. It would never have occurred to an ancient Jew that a man could belong to the one without belonging to the other, for the Church was the State and the State was the Church.

---

[1]   Halsbury, *Laws of England*, 4th ed., vol. 14, para. 345. The 4th ed. is referred to throughout.

There was a single theocratic entity. The law was held to be divine, and concerned itself equally with matters of religious observance and with taxation, with religious orthodoxy and with hygiene,[2] 'Thou shalt have none other Gods but me'; 'thou shalt not make to thyself any graven image', 'six days shalt thou labour . . . but the seventh day is the Sabbath . . . in it thou shalt do no manner of work, thou and thy son, and thy daughter, thy man-servant and thy maid-servant, thy cattle, and the stranger that is within thy gates'; 'thou shalt do no murder'; 'thou shalt not commit adultery; 'thou shalt not steal'; 'thou shalt not bear false witness'. Here, in the one basic code of the Ten Commandments which formed the root of the Levitical law, are put both the fundamentals of religion and also, springing from them, labour laws, regulations affecting immigrants, laws for the protection of animals, laws concerning sexual morality, and the ordinary criminal prohibitions against homicide, larceny, and perjury to be found in most communities. There was no law which was not regarded as divine, and there was no facet of the national religion which was not regarded as part of the law.

In England we find neither that aloofness of the law towards religion which characterizes the American approach nor that complete identification of Church and State which characterized ancient Jewry. If modern England in practice approximates more nearly to the American concept, ancient England approximated more nearly to the Jewish one. But, whereas in ancient Jewry there was an identification of Church and State, in England it was more in the nature of a marriage between the two, with the further characteristic of marriage that the two parties retained their individual characteristics, but were regarded for many purposes as one.

By the time of the Conquest the identification was close. The bishop and the sheriff and the earldorman sat together in the Shire Court; and the bishop or archdeacon (or at one time the parish priest) sat with the town reeve in the Hundred Court.[3] The personnel of these two courts was thus clerical and secular and the work which they did was indifferently secular and

---

2. See. e.g., Leviticus i. 3; ii. 7; xiii; xiiiv. 16; xxvii. 30 and 31.
3. This not to say that there were no purely ecclesiastical tribunals. The position in this respect is not clear.

ecclesiastical. So close an identification between Church and
State in the administration of justice did not appeal to William
the Conqueror, and by the year 1072 he had separated the
Church courts from the temporal courts, assigning spiritual
causes to the one and secular causes to the other.

But this separation did not provide anything like the neat
dichotomy which the modern reader might expect. As has been
observed,[4] cases concerning advowsons (or the right of
ecclesiastical patronage) were soon effectively claimed by the
king for his secular courts, while defamation was recognized as
an ecclesiastical offence within the cognizance of the
ecclesiastical courts. Nor was it till the nineteenth century that
probate matters and matrimonial causes were removed from the
ecclesiastical courts, coming ultimately to rest in the new
Probate, Divorce and Admiralty Division of the High Court of
Justice, the predecessor of the Family Division. Furthermore,
although before long there were two bodies of lawyers, the
common lawyers in the Inns of Court, and the ecclesiastical
lawyers who eventually formed Doctors' Commons, there were
nevertheless many with a knowledge of both systems of law, and
ecclesiastics were to be found in many posts of secular
responsibility, both administrative and legal. Among the most
important of these was the King's Chancellor (eventually to be
known as the Lord Chancellor), who in his Court of Chancery
and in his ecclesiastical capacity as Keeper of the King's
Conscience administered that parallel system of secular law
called equity which owed much of its inspiration to the
theological background of its dispenser. To all this must be
added the fact that in Parliament the Lords spiritual
outnumbered the Lords temporal, and that throughout the land
only one religion was recognized and none other tolerated.

If, then, in medieval England the Establishment may be
likened to a marriage between Church and State, with the
Reformation the union became even closer, approximating
more nearly to the ancient Jewish conception of complete
identification. Before the Reformation, Church and State
existed side by side in a large measure of marital harmony,
though with some matrimonial tensions. Each recognized the

---

[4]   See p. 4 ante.

authority of the other within its own sphere, though disputes might arise as to the delimitation of the two spheres. The king's courts were the king's courts, administering the king's law. The Church's courts were the Church's courts, administering the Church's law.[5] Everyone in England was equally under both. But at the Reformation, with the king now the Supreme Governor on Earth of the Church of England, the Church's courts became beyond dispute the king's courts, and the Church's law was not merely enforced on Englishmen, but was beyond dispute a part of the king's law. Much went on as it had done for centuries. The common law of England and the *jus commune* of the Church still formed the basis of the law administered throughout the land, and the common law courts and the ecclesiastical courts still divided the work between them, much as before; but henceforth the authority of both sets of courts stemmed from the king, and the law which each administered was to be without doubt the law of the land, and the ultimate authority for altering the law, whether secular or ecclesiastical, was to be the King in Parliament, and the procedure for altering it was by Act of Parliament. It is this identification of Church and State which is the essential mark of Establishment. It can exist with or without toleration for those who do not wish to conform. In England for some centuries, both before and after the Reformation, in matters of religion the country might properly be described as totalitarian, though by no means always fanatical. Only the official religion received recognition and deviations from it were liable to bring the deviationists into conflict with the law. The history of the last three centuries has shown an increasing recognition of liberty of conscience, and today, with a few very minor exceptions, no obstacles are placed in the way of those who wish to practise or promote a religion other than that of the Church of England.[6] But it is only within the Established Church that the officials of the Church are officials of the State; that the governmental organs of the Church are governmental organs of the State; and that the Church's judges are as much the Queen's judges as are

---

5.   Lord Blackburn would probably have held that the Church's law was part of the law of England, even before the Reformation. See his observations in *Mackonochie v. Lord Penzance*, [1881] 6 App. Cas. 424, at p.446.

6.   See Chapter XVI *post*.

the secular judges, with their decrees enforced by the machinery of the State.

The situation is reciprocal. It is only the Established Church which has to recognize the organs of the State as organs of the Church; which finds a good deal of its law in the decisions of secular courts; and which must look to the Queen in Parliament as the effective supreme authority in the ordering of its affairs.

But here a word of caution is needed. It must not be thought than an unestablished religion is free from State control. Still less is this the case with a disestablished religion, the Church in Wales, for example. No body or person anywhere in the world is or can be free from the authority of the prince, whether the prince be a monarch or an assembly or any other form of supreme secular authority. The disestablished Church in Wales has to look to its instrument of disestablishment, the Welsh Church Act, 1914,[7] and cannot depart from its provisions. The unestablished Salvation Army had to have its constitution interpreted and its decisions anulled by the Chancery Division in litigation in 1929. The affairs of the 'Wee Frees' in Scotland required an Act of Parliament to regulate them.[8] A Free Church is free only in so far as the supreme secular authority is content to leave it alone, and an Established Church is bound only in so far as the supreme secular authority chooses to exert itself in the Church's affairs. While the identification of Church and State is the mark of Establishment, it is by no means necessarily an indication of the extent to which the one intervenes in the affairs of the other. In Scotland, for example, the Established Kirk is left by Parliament to its own devices to an extent which is the envy of many churchmen in England.

Interference, too, is not all from the side of the secular arm and does not necessarily depend on whether or not there is an established religion. If the countries behind the Iron Curtain provide examples of a measure of control by the State over the affairs of unestablished and disestablished religious bodies, Malta and Spain provide examples of the influence which an Established Church can bring to bear on secular affairs, and

---

[7].   4 & 5 Geo. V, c.91. See Chapter XVI *post*.

[8].   Churches (Scotland) Act, 1905 (5 Edw. VII, c.12). This followed litigation which went to the House of Lords in *Free Church of Scotland* v. *Lord Overtoun and others* (1904), A.C. 515.

Eire provides an example of a similar influence by an unestablished Church. Various facets of the Establishment in England will meet with the approval of some and with the disapproval of others. It is worth remembering that these same facets can be presented outside an Establishment and can be avoided within one. We are concerned here only with an exposition of what in fact exists, and that is sufficient to provide much food for thought, for it will be found that, for good or for ill, the effects of the Establishment permeate most aspects of the Church of England and many aspects of English secular life.

III

THE CONSTITUTION: (II)
ECCLESIASTICAL

The *laos* or people of God form that part of the Church which is militant here in earth. All of them should be called *the laity*, but by long usage the term has come to be applied to that vastly larger part of the *laos* which is not ordained. The smaller part consists of those who have received ordination into the three-fold sacred ministry. 'It is evident unto all men diligently reading Holy Scripture and ancient Authors, that from the Apostles' time there have been these Orders of Ministers in Christ's Church; Bishops, Priests and Deacons.' So has run the Preface to the Ordinal in the Book of Common Prayer for 300 years, undeterred by the fact that the Established Kirk of Scotland, the Free Churches in England, and most continental Protestants have found it so far from evident that they have based their life and worship on a different assumption. But, evident or not, it is a tenet of the Catholic Church, both Western and Orthodox, and, as such, is shared by that part of the Catholic Church established in England. It is sometimes claimed that there is a third category of person within the total *laos*, namely the *persona mixta*, of whom the outstanding example is the Sovereign. But this is a refinement which need not delay us. The officials of the Church are to be found among those who have been ordained and those who have not, and, indeed, having regard to the nature of the Establishment, those who are not even Christians may have some say in the affairs of the Church, for example in the two Houses of Parliament. It is with the rights and duties of all these persons that a book on the law of the Church is concerned, and, having had a glance at the framework of the Establishment, it is convenient next to look at the constitutional structure within that framework.

The basic unit of the Church is the diocese with the bishop at the head of it. The dioceses are grouped together into provinces with an archbishop at the head. Each diocese is divided into parishes and the parishes are grouped together into rural deaneries and the rural deaneries are grouped together into archdeaconries. This may sound confusing; but, according to Anglican thought, it puts the theological emphasis in the right place, namely, on the diocese; *ubi episcopus, ibi ecclesia*. The parish priest, though now possessed of many rights, is in origin only the deputy of the bishop, who, as incumbent paramount, has the cure of all the souls in his diocese. The rural deaneries and archdeaconries are only for administrative convenience, as is also the grouping together of the dioceses into a province. In the Western Catholic Church, as the power of the pope increased, the tendency grew to place the emphasis on Rome, and to regard all authority as stemming from the centre; *ubi Petrus, ibi ecclesia*. The archbishops in their provinces were regarded more and more as his deputies, and the diocesan bishops were called the suffragans of the archbishop. The Reformation made no immediate difference in this respect; it was simply that the main emphasis shifted from the pope to the king, and soon to the King in Parliament. But the Reformation did direct men's minds towards a study of the primitive Church, and it is as a result of this study that theologically, if not jurisprudentially, the Anglican emphasis today tends to be on the bishop and diocese. But as a matter of convenience, it is simpler to begin by saying that, under the Queen, England is divided into the two provinces of Canterbury and York, each with its archbishop; that each province contains a number of dioceses, each with its bishop; that each diocese has one or more archdeaconries; that each archdeaconry has several rural deaneries; and that each rural deanery is made up of a number of parishes. It is still, however, convenient to consider first the position and function of the bishop in his diocese.

Bishops must be at least 30 years old[1] and are appointed by the Sovereign on the advice of the Prime Minister of the day, but are consecrated by other bishops. Upon a vacancy, a standing committee set up by the Church provides a short list of two names to the Prime Minister, who retains the right to

---

[1]   Act of Uniformity, 1662 (14 Car. II, c.4), Canon C2 and the Ordinal. For a priest the minimum age is 24 and for a deacon it is 23: see the Ordinal and Canon C3.

recommend either name to the Sovereign, or to ask the committee for a further name or names. This procedure was adopted in 1976, and since it does not curtail the Crown's powers of appointment no legislation was required to put it into effect. Provision has, however, been made for the establishment for every diocese of the requisite committee, known as the Vacancy in See Committee.[2] The normal method of appointment is that the Crown sends *a congé d'élire*, that is, a licence under the Great Seal, to the chapter of the cathedral church of the diocese, giving the chapter leave to elect a bishop. But the *congé d'élire* is accompanied by a letter missive which contains only one name, namely, that of the Crown's nominee. If within twelve days the chapter does not elect the person named, the Crown may appoint its nominee by letters patent, and the members of the chapter were, at least in theory, liable to the penalties of *praemunire*, which included being put outside the Queen's protection, forfeiture, and imprisonment at the Queen's pleasure.[3] The next step is the purely formal, quasi-judicial one of confirmation of the election by the judge who is known as the vicar general of the province. Though objectors may be heard, there are only two valid grounds of objection. One is that there has been some defect in the method of election. The other is that the person before the vicar general is not the person of the Crown's choice. The person named takes the oath of allegiance to the Crown and that of obedience to the archbishop, and he thereupon becomes in law the bishop of the diocese. But, if he has never been consecrated bishop, before he can perform the sacramental acts of a bishop he must first be consecrated. This requires three bishops, and is normally performed by the archbishop, who acts under mandate from the Crown, with the assistance of a number[4] of other bishops. If the archbishop were to refuse to consecrate the Crown's

---

[2] The Vacancy in See Committees Regulation 1977. The Prime Minister's Secretary for Appointments and the Archbishop's Secretary for Appointments must be invited to attend committee meetings.

[3] Appointments of Bishops Act, 1533 (25 Hen. VIII, c.20), and Statute of Praemunire, 1392 (16 Ric. II, c.5). The offences of *praemunire*, of which there were several, have now been abolished; see the Criminal Law Act 1967 (15 & 16 Eliz. II, c.58).

[4] Usually many more than two other bishops.

nominee, he too would in theory have been liable to the penalties of *praemunire*. After consecration (if consecration is required), the new bishop pays homage to the Queen for his temporalities.[5] After that he is enthroned in his cathedral church.

Legislation[6] is in the course of enactment which will make important alterations to the form of episcopal appointment. Election and confirmation are to be abolished. In their place, as a preliminary to consecration and enthronement, the Crown's nomination will be received and recorded by the archbishop of the province. At the same time the person nominated will give his consent to be bishop, take the oaths of allegiance and of obedience, and be vested with the appropriate spiritualities. A declaration will thereupon be made that he is bishop of the vacant see.

The bishop is the chief minister in the diocese. He has his throne or *cathedra* in his cathedral church, over which, however, he has considerably less authority than he has over the parish churches in the diocese, by reason of the fact that the cathedral is governed by a dean (or provost) and chapter in accordance with the cathedral's statutes, which confer upon them a large measure of autonomy. The bishop alone (or by another bishop deputed by him) ordains priests (though other priests present take part in the laying on of hands); the bishop alone (or by another bishop deputed by him) makes deacons, confirms the baptized, and consecrates land and buildings. He appoints the chancellor of the diocese and the archdeacons, the honorary canons of the cathedral church, and the rural deans. The appointment of the residentiary canons is usually his; he is nearly always the patron of many of the livings in the diocese, and appoints to other livings when the patronage lapses by reason of the failure of the patrons to make an appointment. He has multifarious duties and rights, some of which will be treated of later.

To the bishop belongs the general oversight of the diocese.

---

5. Revenues etc.
6. To have become the Appointment of Bishops Measure 1984. The proposed measure was in fact rejected by the House of Commons on 17 July 1984. It is uncertain whether further attempts will be made to alter the existing law.

This is for the most part conducted as part of the day-to-day business; but from time to time it is exercised by a formal visitation, whether of the cathedral or of the diocese or of a part of it. By canon law this is to be 'at times and places limited by law or custom'[7] but in practice it tends to be a rare event. A formal visitation partakes of the nature of the court. It is usually preceded by the distribution of articles of inquiry directed to the cathedral chapter, parish priests, and churchwardens, and containing a number of questions the answers to which are of interest to the bishop. Usually certain centres are selected by the bishop to which he summons the clergy and churchwardens and others, and there he delivers a charge in the form of an address. Formerly the visitation was an occasion for taking disciplinary action against persons subject to ecclesiastical law; but, with the growth of statutory provision for dealing with such cases by more normal legal process, this has become almost a thing of the past. Visitations have, in consequence, lost much of their edge, and have become simply a more formal method of acquainting the bishop with what is going on and of providing a slightly spectacular means by which he launches his ideas upon the diocese.

If a diocesan bishop wishes to have the assistance of a suffragan bishop, he asks the Crown to appoint one. Where the proposed appointment is a new one, or the suffragan bishop's see has been vacant for five years or more, the diocesan bishop may only petition the Crown after he has secured the approval of the Diocesan Synod and the General Synod.[8] If his petition is granted, he has in effect the choice of whom to appoint. He must submit two names to the Queen, who in practice appoints the person first named and directs the archbishop to consecrate him (unless he is already a bishop) and assigns to him a titular see within the province.[9] The bishop further has an unfettered discretion to appoint any bishop (for example, a retired bishop) as assistant bishop. But neither a suffragan nor an assistant bishop takes any more authority than the diocesan bishop chooses to bestow on him.

[7] Canon G5. The visitation of a cathedral will in future be regulated by the cathedrals statutes, made in pursuance of the Cathedrals Measure, 1963 (No. 2).

[8] Dioceses Measure 1978 (No.1) s.18.

[9] Suffragan Bishops Act, 1534 (26 Hen. VIII, c.14).

A bishop may retire (and must retire on reaching the age of 70[10]) by tendering his resignation to the Queen through the archbishop, or he may be made to retire if he is incapacitated, physically or mentally, from performing the duties of his office. This can occur only under the Bishops (Retirement) Measure, 1951,[11] which applies to archbishops, diocesans, and suffragans, and it requires the concurrence of three diocesan bishops appointed by the Upper House of the relevant Convocation. The bishop may demand a medical examination. If, however, the verdict of the three bishops and of the archbishop is unfavourable, he may be requested to resign, and, if he fails to do so, the archbishop may declare the see vacant, but such a declaration requires to be confirmed by the Queen in Council. Similar provisions exist in the case of the incapacity of an archbishop, the two senior bishops of the province playing the part assigned to an archbishop where a bishop's capacity is in question.[12]

It is upon the archdeacon, within his archdeaconry, that the daily supervision of the parishes falls. He also may hold a visitation and in fact does so once a year at which he admits new churchwardens, usually delivers a charge, and investigates the affairs of each parish by means of articles of inquiry. It is also one of his duties to examine candidates for ordination.

Within an archdeaconry the parishes are grouped into rural deaneries. The rural dean is appointed by the bishop and holds his unremunerative office at the bishop's pleasure. He has few statutory duties, but is in practice called upon to assist the archdeacon and advise the parochial clergy in a large number of matters.

Finally, in the operational scale, we come to the operational unit itself—the parish with its parish priest, churchwardens, Parochial Church Council, and the persons for whom it all exists, namely, the parishioners. But it will be convenient to leave the study of the parish till later.

Before leaving the diocese, mention must be made of the Diocesan Synod, a body established in each diocese by the

---

[10.] Ecclesiastical Offices (Age Limit) Measure 1975 (No.2).

[11.] No.2.

[12.] A new Bishops (Retirement) Measure is in the course of enactment, which will modify in some respects the procedure described in the text.

Synodical Government Measure 1969[13] and consisting of a House of Bishops, a House of Clergy, and a house of Laity. A House of Bishops consists of the diocesan bishop, every suffragan bishop of the diocese, and such other person or persons in episcopal orders working in the diocese as the bishop of the diocese may nominate. The House of Clergy usually consists of clergymen elected by each House of Clergy of every Deanery Synod in the diocese, together with certain *ex officio* members, some co-opted by the House of Clergy of the Diocesan Synod, and some appointed by the bishop. The House of Laity consists of laymen and laywomen elected by the House of Laity of the Deanery Synod, together with some *ex officio* members, some co-opted by the House of Laity itself, and some appointed by the bishop. The Diocesan Synod must meet not less than twice a year. It is primarily a deliberative body, but has gradually acquired a variety of specific powers. Perhaps its most important functions are in connection with the repair of benefice buildings, the ultimate control of the Diocesan Board of Finance; the appointment of persons to serve on important committees such as the Pastoral Committee; and the making of provision for the membership and procedure of Deanery Synods. Deanery Synods were introduced by the Synodical Government Measure 1969 as an intermediate body between the Diocesan Synod, and the Parochial Church Councils operating within the parishes. Their membership, of not more than 150 nor (if practicable) less than 50, is divided into Houses of Clergy and Laity. Their primary function is to provide a forum for discussion, but their powers may be extended by the General Synod.

Now that we have glanced at the structure of the basic unit, the diocese, we can turn to an examination of the larger structure of which the diocese is but a part.

Within the Catholic Church of Christ is an autonomous branch established in England, and at the top of it comes the Queen in Parliament, 'over all persons in all causes, as well ecclesiastical as temporal, throughout her dominions

---

[13.] See in particular the Church Representation Rules, enacted as Schedule 3 of the Synodical Government Measure 1969 (No.2) but subsequently revised and amended.

supreme'.[14] The Queen, Lords, and Commons together form the sovereign power and can in law legislate for Church and State as they wish. In fact, much of the Church's legislation has been and still is by Act of Parliament, and the Queen, acting on the advice of the Ministers of the Crown, has a wide ecclesiastical patronage (including the appointment of bishops) and many executive functions, often exercised by Order in Council under statutory authority. All other persons and bodies are, in law, subordinate to the overriding sovereignty of the Queen in Parliament. Many members of each House of Parliament are, of course, members of the Church of England, though many are not. Clerks in holy orders may not be members of the House of Commons; but twenty-six bishops sit in the House of Lords, namely, the Archbishops of Canterbury and York, the Bishops of London, Durham, and Winchester, and twenty-one other bishops in order of their seniority by appointment to an English diocese.

England is divided into the two provinces of Canterbury and York, each with its archbishop, each of whom, as well as being archbishop of the province, is respectively bishop of the diocese of Canterbury and of the diocese of York.

Each province has its ancient parliament, called Convocation, claiming an origin older than that of the Parliament of the realm. Originally in England, as on the Continent, Convocation was a gathering of prelates, but in the thirteenth century it became in England what it has remained ever since, a gathering both of bishops and of the inferior clergy. It was in Convocation that the contribution of the clergy to the royal exchequer was voted, and, though Edward I wished for a transfer of this function to Parliament, the clergy, nevertheless, continued to tax themselves in Convocation until 1664.

Each Convocation consists of an Upper House of all the diocesan bishops in the province together with a number of suffragan bishops,[15] and of a Lower House of the inferior clergy. Some of these, called proctors, are the elected representatives of the clergy in the dioceses and in the universities of Oxford, Cambridge, London, Durham, and Newcastle; in each province one representative is elected by the

---

[14.] Bidding Prayer.   [15.] Canon H3.

remaining universities there. In the Lower House also sit representatives of the deans and provosts of each cathedral; and archdeacon from each diocese; a representative of the clerical members of the religious communities in the province; and certain *ex officio* members. There is also provision for co-opting members.[16] Suffragan bishops are no longer entitled to sit in the Lower House or participate in elections to it. Unless the Sovereign appoints a Vicegerent (which has never happened since Henry VIII appointed Cromwell), the archbishop is the president and presides in the Upper House and at joint meetings of both Houses, and the Lower House elects one of its number as prolocutor, and he acts as chairman of that House.

The Thirty-nine Articles state[17] that 'General Councils may not be gathered together without the commandment and will of Princes', and although Convocation is not a General Council, something of the spirit of this Article has always been present to the minds of English monarchs. Provincial synods were in medieval times summoned under the authority of the pope for purely ecclesiastical business. But Convocation was peculiar to England and parallel to the secular Parliament and its decisions were of direct interest to the king, at least in so far as taxation of the clergy was concerned. It met, therefore, only in response to a royal writ,[18] and the same is true today. Formerly, when the Queen issued writs for the summoning of Parliament, she also issued writs to the two archbishops, on the strength of which they issued mandates for the summoning of Convocation. The life of Convocation was indeed, linked with that of Parliament. Convocation was thought to be dissolved automatically with the dissolution of Parliament. The link between the duration of Parliament and Convocation has, however, now been broken. Convocation may be called together and dissolved at such times as the Queen may determine, without regard to the time at which Parliament is summoned or dissolved.[19] In the days when Parliament stood dissolved on the demise of the Crown, Convocation also stood

---

16. This is only a brief summary of the composition of Convocation, full details of which are set out in Canons H2 and H3.

17. Article XXI.

18. This was the case at any rate towards the end of the pre- Reformation period.

19. Church of England Convocations Act 1966 (14 & 15 Eliz. II. c.2)

dissolved; but today, when, by statute, Parliament no longer stands dissolved on the demise of the Crown,[20] Convocation also continues as though undissolved, though the Acts make no mention of Convocation.

It would be hard to say with precision what were the limits to the authority of Convocation before the Tudors; but this would be true of any other constitutional organ in the days when they were all evolving. After the submission of the Clergy Act 1533,[21] its legislative business was confined to the passing of canons. To discuss their business the royal licence was required, and no canon became effective until it had received the royal assent. If it did receive the royal assent, it became effective in the province which passed it. It was thus possible for the two provinces to have different canons. With the transfer to the General Synod of the power to make canons Convocation has lost its residual legislative power.[22] Canons enacted by the General Synod extend to both provinces.

Apart from legislative matters, Convocation has felt itself free to discuss a wide variety of topics and to pass resolutions thereon. These resolutions, though in themselves devoid of legal effect, nevertheless carry great weight in matters of theological import and ecclesiastical polity and are of evidential value in courts of law as indicating the mind of the Church and thereby throwing light on points of doctrine. This is especially the case when Convocation dignifies a resolution by calling it an 'act of Convocation'.

In May 1919 the two Convocations took a step of very great importance to the Church of England. They presented Addresses to the King as a result of which the Church of England Assembly (Powers) Act, 1919, was passed by Parliament. This Act, commonly called the Enabling Act, incorporated the Appendix to the Addresses of the two Convocations, and gave statutory recognition to a body, already in existence and the creation of the Church itself, the full title of which was the National Assembly of the Church of England, commonly known as the Church Assembly. The

[20].   Representation of the People Act, 1867 (30 & 31 Vict., c.102), s.51.
[21].   25 Hen. VIII, c.19.
[22].   See p.7 *ante*.

effect of this Act was to bestow a large measure of legislative authority upon the Church Assembly, far greater than any authority which the Convocations had ever possessed, for a Measure of the Church Assembly acquired the full force of an Act of Parliament.

In 1970 the Church Assembly was renamed the General Synod of the Church of England and became part of the comprehensive scheme of synodical government created by the Synodical Government Measure 1969.

The General Synod consists of three Houses namely: (1) the House of Bishops, consisting of the members of the Upper Houses of the two Convocations (including the elected suffragan bishops[23]); (2) the House of Clergy, consisting of the members of the Lower Houses of the two Convocations; and (3) the House of Laity, consisting of actual communicant laymen and laywomen elected in each diocese, by electors,[24] together with one member from each province chosen by the lay members of religious communities from among their number, *ex officio* members (not exceeding seven) and co-opted members (not exceeding five). The composition of the House of Bishops and the House of Clergy is thus identical with the composition of the two Convocations at any given moment. Elections to the House of Laity normally occur every five years or when there is a casual vacancy. Because of the presence of the laity the General Synod is easily the most representative body in the Church of England and for that reason probably carries the most weight as well as possessing the greatest legislative authority after Parliament. The question is indeed sometimes raised as to whether there is any point in the continued existence of the two Convocations. They have, however, survived, partly because of a reluctance to abolish institutions which are older than Parliament, partly from a fear lest, if they went, the larger southern province would by force of numbers swamp the smaller northern province, and partly from recognition of the fact that the clergy, like every professional body, need a purely professional forum in which to exchange views.

[23.] See Canon H3.

[24.] The diocesan electors are the members of the Houses of Laity of all the deanery synods in each diocese.

The General Synod normally meets for the inside of a week three times a year. It may meet more often and is bound to meet at least twice a year. The Archbishop of Canterbury and the Archbishop of York are joint Presidents; if neither Archbishop wishes to take the chair, a member of a panel of chairmen, elected by the Synod, does so. The three Houses may meet separately or together and both courses are followed, though in practice most of the business is done in joint session. No Measure or Canon can be passed unless it is passed in all three Houses, and, if they are sitting together, any twenty-five members may demand or vote by Houses. If a Measure concerns doctrine or services or ceremonies, it must be debated and voted by each of the Houses separately and finally put to the Synod for acceptance or rejection in the form proposed by the House of Bishops; the Synod may not make any statement purporting to define a doctrine, or encroach on the functions of the episcopacy.[25] In certain cases the provisions of the constitution of the General Synod or of a Measure require special majorities of the Synod or each of its constituent houses.

With these modifications, the authority of the Synod is very wide, having regard to the fact that its Measures have the full effect of Acts of Parliament and may even repeal Acts of Parliament. But Parliament has not relinquished its claim to the ultimate control over the affairs of the Church. A Measure does not become effective until it has received the royal assent, and the royal assent cannot be given unless each House of Parliament has passed a resolution that the Measure should be presented to the Queen. The General Synod has a Legislative Committee and Parliament has an Ecclesiastical Committee consisting of members of both Houses. The two Committees have liaison with each other as a result of which Measures are sometimes withdrawn by the Synod instead of being placed before Parliament. But every Measure which reaches Parliament is accompanied by a report of the Ecclesiastical Committee as to its effect and the Committee's views thereon,

---

[25]. It may be that as part of a scheme of true synodical government involving bishops, inferior clergy, and laity, these limitations will go. They exist at present in order to protect the bishops in their historical position as the guardians of the faith and in an attempt not to trespass too far on the functions of the Convocation.

with particular regard to the constitutional rights of the Queen's subjects.

The fact that the power to make canons has passed from Convocation to the General Synod does not affect the statutory requirements of royal licence and royal assent enshrined in the submission of the Clergy Act, 1533.[26] Neither has there been any alteration in the limited legal effect of canons.[27] A canon is of no effect if it is repugnant to the general law of the land, whether common law or statutory. Furthermore, it is in itself not binding on anyone except clerics, or, at least, ecclesiastical *personae*.

It should be added that the General Synod has many boards and committees of considerable importance, such as the Central Board of Finance, the Church's Advisory Council for the Ministry, and the Legal Advisory Commission, and that it frequently appoints *ad hoc* committees (confined to members of the Synod) or commissions (not so confined). The work of these committees and commissions often results in legislation. With the notable exception of the rejection by Parliament of the proposed Revised Prayer Book in 1927 and 1928, clashes between Parliament and the Assembly or its successor have been avoided, largely owing to the good offices of the Legislative Committee and the Ecclesiastical Committee and to a desire on both sides to avoid a situation which might in practice lead to disestablishment. Members of both Houses of Parliament have, however, frequently exerted their undoubted legal rights to discuss Measures of the General Synod, and members of the General Synod are seldom unconscious for long that in anything which they propose parliamentary control and the royal prerogative are very real factors which must be taken into account.

It remains now in this chapter to consider the two provinces of Canterbury and York, each with its own archbishop or metropolitan.

The archbishop of the province is also bishop of his own diocese. His appointment, like that of any other bishop, is in the hands of the Queen, acting on the advice of the Prime Minister,

---

[26]   See p.6 *ante*.

[27]   Synodical Government Measure 1969 (No.2) Sch. 2, art. 6(a)(ii).

and is substantially by the same procedure, save that in the case of the Archbishopric of Canterbury the committee meets under the chairmanship of a lay communicant Anglican appointed by the Prime Minister. The Queen sends a *congé d'élire* to the dean and chapter of the metropolitical cathedral church, accompanied by a letter missive containing the name of the person to be elected. The confirmation of the election is by the other archbishop and two bishops or alternatively by four other bishops, and consecration (if the nominee is not already a bishop) is by them.

As bishop of his own diocese, the archbishop may, of course, visit the diocese. But as archbishop he may carry out a visitation anywhere within his province, and all the bishops and other clergy in the province are subject to his visitation. Archiepiscopal visitations have become rare in modern times, and it has long been customary for the Archbishop of Canterbury not to visit the diocese of London. The archbishop's position in his own Convocation and in the General Synod has already been noted.[28] During a vacancy in a see in his province the archbishop acts as guardian of the spiritualities,[29] and as such institutes to livings, and when the see is filled, it is normally the archbishop who, if necessary, consecrates the new bishop.[30] In the Diocese of Durham, however, the Dean and Chapter claim the guardianship of the spiritualities during a vacancy and in fact exercise it, though the claim is formally denied by the Archbishop of York. During a vacancy in a metropolitical see, the dean and chapter of the metropolitical cathedral church are the guardians of the spiritualities.[31]

The Archbishop of Canterbury is known as the Primate of All England and the Archbishop of York as Primate of England. Their functions as archbishop, each within his own province, are the same; but the Archbishop of Canterbury has additional functions. He is the generally acknowledged, though unofficial,

---

28. p.23. Some of his many other functions are noted in later chapters.
29. Canon C19(2). In most cases the archbishop has acquired prescriptive rights to the guardianship of the spiritualities.
30. See p.20 *ante*.
31. Canon C19(1). Not all cathedral chapters would agree with the statement of law in the text. Claims to the guardianship of the spiritualities have given rise to a number of disputes—an indication that the law is not clear.

leader of the whole Anglican Communion. He is also by statute[32] the inheritor of the ancient legatine powers formerly exercised under the pope's authority, and in the exercise of these powers he is not confined to his own province. It is by virtue of these powers that the Archbishop of Canterbury's special licence for marriages is valid throughout England, that he grants the so-called Lambeth degrees, and gives certain faculties and dispensations.

We can now take stock of the situation. One can regard the constitutional structure of the Church of England either administratively or legislatively or judicially.[33]

Regarded administratively, we find the Queen at the top, acting on the advice of her Ministers of State, with a variety of administrative functions to perform, some of which will be noted later, many of them exercised by Order in Council, and with the important task of finally choosing the bishops and exercising other patronage. Under the Queen we have the two archbishops, each in his own province, exercising oversight over the dioceses. Under the archbishop we have the bishops, each in his own diocese exercising oversight over the parishes; each bishop being assisted in this task by the division of his diocese into archdeaconries, each with its archdeacon; the archdeaconries being themselves subdivided into the rural deaneries into which the parishes are grouped.

Regarded legislatively, the supreme, sovereign legislature is the Queen in Parliament, able in law to do anything by Act of Parliament. Parallel, but subordinate to Parliament, are the ancient Convocations, now shorn of all effective legislative power. Also subordinate to Parliament is the General Synod, with its extensive right to legislate for the whole country by Measures approved by Parliament and assented to by the Queen.

If it is thought that undue emphasis has here been placed on the authority of the Crown and of Parliament, it must be remembered that legally this is inevitable, as in strict law it reflects the position. But it should be remembered that Dicey[34]

---

32. Ecclesiastical Licences Act, 1533 (25 Hen. VIII, c.21).
33. The judicial structure is to be found in Chapter XIV.
34. The Law of the Constitution.

draws a distinction between the legal sovereign, who in law can do anything, and the political sovereign, who in law may be able to do nothing but in practice can sometimes do everything, and in this context he contrasts the legal sovereignty of Parliament with the political sovereignty of the electorate. In the affairs of the Church of England it may not be easy to pinpoint the political sovereign, but it can confidently be stated that all political sovereignty does not reside in the legal sovereign. Churchmen are conscious of the fact that the Church of England is but a part of the larger whole, the Catholic Church which is the Body of Christ, and that she can be true to her mission only in so far as she conforms to the mind of her Founder. There are, therefore, some things which cannot be accepted, and this is known to the individuals, churchmen and others, who go to make up the sovereign Parliament as well as to those legislators, parishioners, clerics, and others, who together form the visible Church on earth. These thoughts provide a moderating influence which, although outside the realm of law, cannot be and are not ignored.

IV

THE PARISH

For most Englishmen today the Church means primarily the parish church—the place to which they go for worship, if they go anywhere, and the unit in which, for matters of religion, they live and move and have their being. It was not always so. The cathedral was the parish church, the bishop was the pastor, and the diocese was his *parochia*. He gathered round him priests and deacons and sent out some of them on his behalf to outlying districts. Then, as Christianity spread, permanent churches sprang up to serve those districts remote from the cathedral. Sometimes these churches were built by local notables, and then it was natural that they should have an effective voice in the choice of a priest to serve the church. Sometimes, with the increase in monasticism, a religious house would provide a church to serve the needs of a district, and the religious house would put in a priest to look after it. But the bishop was still the pastor of the whole *parochia* or diocese and responsible for the care of all the souls in it. Thus grew up the system which we know today—the system of private patronage in which both the patron of the church and the bishop are concerned in the appointment of the parish priest, with, as it has turned out, the scales weighted heavily in favour of the patron.

In course of time these churches acquired property for the maintenance of the priest. Sometimes this took the form of glebeland, off which the priest lived. The generous faithful would endow a church, and all the faithful (which then meant everybody), whether generous or not, were subject to tithe, whereby a tenth part of their produce went to God, or, rather, was taken by the Church. In the case of those churches where the parson was appointed by a lay patron, he was known as the rector and took the greater tithes. But in the case of those churches which had been provided by a religious community, that community was regarded as the rector and consequently took the greater tithes, out of which provision was made for a priest to look after the church as the community's vicar or deputy. This, in very brief outline, is the explanation of the fact that today some parish priests are known as rectors and others as vicars. At the Reformation Henry VIII expropriated monastic property of all sorts, including the right to receive tithe, and rewarded laymen with the spoils. There thus came into existence a number of lay rectors. Meantime the advowson, as the right of patronage was called, had become a saleable commodity, distinct from the right to receive tithe; and so it does not necessarily follow that today a lay rector of a church is also the patron, though that is often the case, nor does it follow that when a religious foundation, such as a cathedral, is today the patron, it is also the rector, for it may have acquired its patronage from a lay source. Tithe is now, by a series of Acts of Parliament,[1] virtually a thing of the past, and advowsons, though transferable, cannot now be sold;[2] but their long history has left its marks, one of which is this distinction between the parson we call rector and the parson we call vicar.[3]

In the Book of Common Prayer is a prayer to God to 'send down upon our Bishops and Curates and all Congregations committed to their charge the healthful Spirit of' his grace. This is a prayer for those with the cure, or care, of souls and for their flocks. It is not a prayer for all the clergy, save in so far as a clergyman without a cure of souls is one of a flock. The bishop has the overall cure of souls throughout his diocese, but to the parish priest (or incumbent) is committed the particular cure of souls within his parish to the exclusion of everyone other than the bishop and those assistants to whom the parish priest may depute some of his responsibility. The parish priest is, therefore, rightly called the curate, while his ordained assistants are only, at most, assistant curates, despite the fact that in modern parlance the assistant curate is the person to whom most people refer as the 'curate'.

In most parishes today there is no assistant curate; but in every parish there are two (or occasionally more) churchwardens, and, since the Enabling Act of 1919 and its

---

1. The Tithe Acts, 1836 to 1925, the Tithe Act, 1936, and the Tithe Act, 1951 (14 & 15 Geo. VI, c.62).
2. Benefices Act, 1898 (Amendment) Measure, 1923 (No. 1)
3. In return for the tithe the lay rector was liable for the upkeep of the chancel. See p. 106 *post*.

consequential legislation,[4] there has been a Parochial Church Council elected at the annual Parochial Church Meeting, and not to be confused with that organ of local government called the Parish Council.

The office of churchwarden is an ancient one, dating from about the thirteenth century. Until recently the ecclesiastical parish was identical with the local government parish, and the churchwardens had a variety of local government functions to perform as well as their ecclesiastical ones. They were, therefore, chosen at a vestry meeting which was normally a meeting of ratepayers for ecclesiastical and local government purposes. Today their former connexion with local government is still shown by the fact that (with a few anomalous and ancient exceptions) they are chosen at a joint session of the ecclesiastical Parochial Church Meeting, the vestry, and the incumbent. Chosen rather than *elected* is the right word. The Churchwardens (Appointment and resignation) Measure 1964 provides that they 'shall be chosen by the joint consent of the minister of the parish and a meeting of the parishioners, if it may be.'[5] In the absence of agreement, or the consent of the minister to the person or persons chosen at the meeting, 'one churchwarden shall be appointed by the minister and the other shall then be elected by the meeting of the parishioners.'[6] In many parishes it seems to be assumed (usually wrongly) that the minister and the parishioners will not agree, and the one announces his choice as 'vicar's warden' and the others proceed to elect their choice as 'people's warden', whereas in fact they should, and, if they knew the law, usually would, have agreed on both candidates. Their functions and standing are identical. They are both admitted to office at the archdeacon's annual visitation or at an episcopal visitation, when they declare that they will faithfully and diligently perform the duties of their office.[7] They are eligible for re-election any number of times and they remain in office until the admission of their successors. By a number of statutes a variety of persons (among them clergymen and barristers) are entitled to claim exemption from

4. See particularly the Synodical Government Measure, 1969 (No.2), and the Church Representation Rules (as amended) made thereunder.
5. Churchwardens (Appointment and Resignation) Measure, 1964 (No.3) s.2(2).
6. S.3.   7. Canon E1(2).

service, while Jews, infants, aliens, and persons convicted of various offences are disqualified from serving. But, unless exempted or disqualified, until recently a person could not (in ancient parishes) refuse to serve, even though not a member of the Church of England. Today, however, he cannot be made a churchwarden without his consent, and (unless the bishop otherwise permits) he must be a communicant member of the Church of England.[8] He may, however, be removed by the Consistory Court for misconduct or he may resign. Upon election, if they are actual communicant members of the Church of England, they become *ex officio* members of the Parochial Church Council, to which body many of their former responsibilities have been transferred.[9] They are still, however, in a special sense at once the representatives of the laity in the parish and the officers of the bishop. With the help of the sidesmen (who are chosen at the annual Parochial Church Meeting) they are responsible for keeping order in the church and churchyard and for the seating of persons in church. The churchwardens are the legal owners of the moveables in the church; they are charged jointly with the incumbent, with the duty of providing the bread and wine used at the Holy Communion; and, together with the incumbent, they decide on the disposal to 'pious and charitable uses' of the alms given at the offertory, 'wherein if they disagree, it shall be disposed of as the Ordinary [that is, the bishop] do appoint'.[10] As *oculi episcopi* it is their duty to report to the bishop any irregularities in the affairs of the parish or in the mode of life of the minister, to make formal presentments, and to answer articles of inquiry at visitations, whether archidiaconal or episcopal. During a vacancy in the living the bishop often appoints the churchwardens as sequestrators to receive the income of the benefice, to make thereout the necessary payments to clergymen for doing duty during the vacancy, and to retain the balance for the new incumbent.

The functions of the Parochial Church Councils include 'co-operation with the incumbent in promoting in the parish the

8. Churchwardens (Appointment and Resignation) Measure, 1964 (No.3).
9. Church Representation Rules, being Schedule 3 to the Synodical Government Measure 1969 (No.2).
10. Rubric in the Book of Common Prayer.

whole mission of the Church, pastoral evangelistic, social and ecumenical'.[11] To the Council are entrusted the finances of the parish and the care and maintenance and insurance of the church and churchyard and of the church's goods, though the legal ownership is not vested in the Council. The Council may frame an annual budget and take steps to raise it, including levying a purely voluntary church rate, and, together with the incumbent, it determines the allocation of collections in church (other than at the offertory) and, with him, may appoint and dismiss a parish clerk, sexton, and others. In those few parishes where the patronage was vested in the parishioners, the Council now is effectively the patron. The services in the church[12] are the joint responsibility of the incumbent and the Council; and by canon[13] the accustomed vesture of the ministers is not to be changed without the agreement of the Council. In practice in many parishes the whole running of the parish has become, as was intended, a co-operative exercise between the incumbent and the Council.[14]

The incumbent is the chairman of the Council,[15] and the vice- chairman, who is elected by the Council, must be a layman. As has been noted, the churchwardens, if communicants, are *ex officio* members of the Council and have jointly to act as treasurer, unless the Council appoints a treasurer. The Council must appoint a member as secretary or, if necessary, engage a paid secretary.

The members must be actual lay communicants aged 16 or upwards, and, if not *ex officio* members, are elected at the annual Parochial Church Meeting and hold office either for one year or for three years, according to the decision of the Meeting, and are eligible for re-election. In addition, the assistant curate (if any, and, if there is more than one, the one nominated by the incumbent), and any lay members of the Deanery Synod, or of the Diocesan Synod, or of the General Synod if on the electoral roll of the parish are *ex officio* members. The Council may also co-opt as members either clerks in Holy Orders or lay

11. Parochial Church Councils (Powers) Measure 1956 (No.3) s.2, as substituted by the Synodical Government Measure, 1969 (No.2) s.6.
12. Canon B 3: see also Canon B 11(2).   13. B.8.
14. By the Inspection of Churches Measure, 1955 (No.1) a duty has also been laid on Diocesan Synods to bring into operation a scheme for a quinquennial architectural inspection of churches in the diocese.
15. Special provisions of the Church Representation Rules (p.34 note 2 *ante*) apply to team ministries.

communicant members aged 16 or upwards provided that the number of persons co-opted does not exceed one-fifth of the number of the elected lay representatives.

Everyone living in the parish is a parishioner regardless of his religious persuasion. So also is anyone who, though not living in the parish, occupies land therein and pays rates. So also is anyone on the electoral roll of the parish. Every baptized parishioner who is sixteen years old or over is entitled to have his name put on the electoral roll, if he declares that he is a member of the Church of England and that he does not belong to any religious body not in communion with the Church of England. So also is any similar person in another parish, provided he has for six months habitually attended public worship in the parish upon whose electoral roll he wishes to be placed. A suitably qualified person may on the roll of two parishes with the consent of the Parochial Church Councils of each parish concerned.

A parishioner, whether or not on the electoral roll, and whether or not a member of the Church of England, has certain obligations and rights.

In strict law he is under an obligation to attend the parish church on all Sundays and holy days unless he has a reasonable excuse for his absence[16] or unless he dissents from the doctrine and worship of the Church and usually attends some place of worship other than that of the Established Church.[17] Attendance at another place of worship of the Church of England is a good excuse,[18] and in any event no pecuniary penalty can be incurred, but only ecclesiastical censure.[19] The Book of Common Prayer[20] further directs that every parishioner shall communicate at least three times a year, of which Easter shall be one; but this must be read together with other rubrics, such as the one which directs that none shall be admitted to the Holy Communion until such time as he be confirmed or be ready and desirous to be confirmed.[21]

As a corollary to his obligation to attend divine worship, a

[16.] Act of Uniformity, 1551 (5 & 6 Edw. VI. c.1)
[17.] Religious Disabilities Act, 1846 (9 & 10 Vict., c.59)
[18.] *Britton* v. *Standish*, [1704] Holt K.B. 141.
[19.] Ibid. Since the passing of the Ecclesiastical Jurisdiction Measure, 1963 (No.1), it would seem that even censure has application only to a clergyman.
[20.] Rubric at the end of the service for Holy Communion.
[21.] Rubric at the end of the Order of Confirmation.

parishioner has a right of entry to the parish church at the time of public worship, so long as there is room for him, standing or sitting, and he has a right to a seat if there is one available, but not a right to any particular seat (unless one has been given him by faculty),[22] and he must sit where directed by the churchwardens. He has a right (if it can be so termed) to the burial of his body in the burial ground of the parish, regardless of his religion. He has a right to be married in the parish church, at any rate if one of the parties to the marriage has been baptized.[23] In general, it is apprehended that, whatever his religion, as a parishioner he has a right to the ministrations of the church, so far as they are appropriate to his condition. Thus, if he be sick, he has a right to the ministrations of the parson, but not to the Communion of the Sick, unless he has been confirmed. It is further apprehended that a temporary visitor to the parish is entitled to the ministrations of the church so far as they are appropriate to his condition; he certainly has the satisfaction of knowing that, if he dies there, he may also be buried there.[24]

To return, however, to the parish priest; we have seen that both the bishop and the patron have a part in his appointment, and it is impossible here to do more than give a bare outline of the considerable body of law on the subject of patronage.[25] On a vacancy's occurring the bishop notifies the patron. The patron then has six months in which to find a successor. If he fails to do so within six months, his right of presentation for that turn lapses to the bishop, though the patron can still exercise his right at any time before the bishop actually makes an appointment; if the bishop fails to provide a successor within six months of the lapse to him, the right lapses to the archbishop, though, again, the patron can still appoint, if he does so before the archbishop; and, if the archbishop too fails to make a presentation within six months, the right lapses to the Crown, and *nullum tempus occurrit rege*. But, if the patron duly presents a priest to the bishop, the bishop is bound to admit him unless he

---

22. See pp.134 et seq.
23. See p.91 *post*.
24. Halsbury, vol. 10, para. 1118.
25. For a detailed account see Halsbury, vol. 13, paras. 776- 831. There are proposals for legislation to modify the law concerning patronage.

has good ground for refusal. A priest who has attained the age of 70 years cannot normally be admitted. Insufficiency of learning on the part of the presentee, immorality, mental or physical incapacity, serious financial embarrassment, neglect of ecclesiastical duty, and simony are among the grounds which justify a bishop in refusing a presentation; but the validity of his refusal can be tested by proper process in the courts, and the bishop can be directed to admit the nominee, and, if he still refuses, the vicar general of the province will do so.[26] The bishop cannot refuse a presentation simply because the person presented is not the person whom the bishop considers suitable; but he has an absolute right to refuse a presentee who was made deacon only within the last three years, or does not have three years, parochial experience.[27] Under the Benefices (Exercise of Rights of Presentation) Measure, 1931,[28] it is possible for a Parochial Church Council to oppose the patron's nominee, and then, in the ultimate resort, it rests with the bishop whether or not to accept him.

The method by which the bishop admits the presentee is by institution into the spiritualities. If the bishop himself is the patron, what would otherwise be called institution is known as collation. In either case, this is followed by induction by the archdeacon or his deputy (often the rural dean) into the actual corporeal possession of the church, during which as a rule the archdeacon places the presentee in physical possession of the church and the presentee marks the fact by ringing the church bell.[29] Although institution may take place anywhere, it is common for institution and induction to take place as part of a service in the parish church. Before admission, the presentee must assent to the Thirty-nine Articles, the Book of Common Prayer, and the Ordinal, and he must also take the oaths of allegiance to the Queen and that of canonical obedience to the bishop.[30]

The presentee is now the incumbent, with the exclusive cure of all the souls in the parish, saving only for the cure which the

[26] Benefices Act, 1898 (61 & 62 Vict., c.48).
[27] Benefices Act, 1898 (61 & 62 Vict., c.48), s.2(1) (b); Canon C10.
[28] No.3.
[29] Canon C11.
[30] Canons C13, C14, and C15; the Promissory Oaths Act, 1868 (31 & 32 Vict., c.72), and the Church of England (Worship and Doctrine) Measure 1974 (No.3).

bishop retains as incumbent paramount. He is a beneficed clergyman, that is, he has a freehold in his parish and enjoys all the benefits thereof until he is required to retire (normally at the age of 70) under the Ecclesiastical Offices (Age Limit) Measure 1975[31] unless he chooses to resign or is removed by due process of law. No one, other than the bishop in person, can lawfully exercise a public ministry within the parish, except with the consent of the incumbent. He must, on pain of forfeiture of his emoluments, reside for nine months of the year in his parish, unless he gets a licence from the bishop to live elsewhere, and his widow may remain in the parsonage house for two months after his death.[32]

Formerly it was said that the incumbent had a freehold, meaning that he might remain in his living for life. Legislation facilitating the removing of incumbents and the reorganization of parishes has eroded a beneficed clergyman's rights to such an extent that it is no longer entirely accurate to describe his office as a freehold. The limitations placed upon the incumbent's traditional freehold rights are considered in the remainder of this chapter.

An incumbent appointed to a benefice after January 1st 1976 is subject to compulsory retirement on attaining the age of 70 years, unless the diocesan bishop considers that there are special circumstances which make it desirable that his retirement should be postponed. Such postponement must have the consent of the Parochial Church Council, and may be for a period not exceeding two years in all.[33] Provision has also been made to remove him in case of 'a serious breakdown of the pastoral relationship' between an incumbent and his parishioners, whether as a result of the incumbent's disability, mental or physical, or owing to the conduct of the incumbent or of his parishioners.[34]

The somewhat complex procedure prescribed in cases of potential pastoral discord is initiated by the incumbent himself, the archdeacon, or a majority of two-thirds of the lay members of the Parochial Church Council, requesting an enquiry into the

[31] No.2.
[32] Pluralities Act 1838 (1 & 2 Vict., c.106); Canon C25.
[33] Ecclesiastical Offices (Age Limit) Measure 1975 (No.2).
[34] Incumbents (Vacation of Benefices) Measure 1977 (No.1).

'pastoral situtation' in the parish. On receipt of the request the diocesan bishop appoints an archdeacon not directly involved in the case to bring about a reconciliation between the incumbent and the parishioners, or if appropriate to recommend the institution of an enquiry. Normally the enquiry will be conducted by a diocesan committee consisting of three clerks in Holy Orders and two lay persons nominated from panels appointed by the Diocesan Synod. The incumbent has, however, the option of referring the matter directly to a provincial tribunal, whose members are unconnected with the diocese in which the parish in question is situated. The chairman of the provincial tribunal is a diocesan chancellor or a Queen's Counsel, and its remaining members are two clerks in Holy Orders and two lay persons. All are appointed by the Vicar-General of the province, who is responsible for constituting the tribunal. The committee or the tribunal is entitled to receive written representations, and to require oral evidence to be given on oath. The incumbent has a right to attend the proceedings, and to give oral evidence, question witnesses, and argue his case. It is the duty of the committee or the tribunal to report to the bishop whether there has been a serious breakdown of the pastoral relationship, and whether the conduct of the incumbent, or of his parishioners, or of both, has contributed to the breakdown; as an alternative there may a finding that the incumbent is unable by reason of age or infirmity of mind or body to discharge adequately the duties attached to his benefice. In the case of a serious breakdown of the pastoral relationship, the bishop may (but only on the recommendation of four or more members of the committee or tribunal) execute a declaration of avoidance declaring the benefice of the incumbent to be vacant; alternatively he may rebuke the incumbent and disqualify him from executing or performing such of the incumbent's rights or duties for such period as the bishop may decide. The bishop also has power to rebuke parishioners if their conduct has contributed to the breakdown, and he may in any event give pastoral advice and guidance to the incumbent and his parishioners.

Where the bishop is satisfied that it is proper to do so, he may direct that a committee of enquiry should be convened solely for the purpose of determining whether an incumbent is unable by reason of age or infirmity of mind or body to discharge adequately his parochial duties. In such circumstances the preliminary procedure adopted in cases of suspected pastoral breakdown is not applicable, and the incumbent cannot elect for the enquiry to be conducted by the provincial tribunal. A committee constituted for this purpose (or a committee or tribunal investigating a possible pastoral breakdown) may report to the bishop that the incumbent is unable adequately to discharge the duties attaching to his benefice by reason of age or infirmity. At least four of its members may also make a recommendation that the incumbent should resign his benefice. When such a recommendation is made the bishop may advise the incumbent to resign and, if he refuses or fails within one month to do so, a declaration of avoidance may be executed. In other cases in which the incumbent is found to be disabled, the bishop is empowered to provide an assistant curate, to give the incumbent up to two years' leave of absence, or to make such other temporary provision as he thinks fit.

Any incumbent removed under this Measure is entitled to compensation for any loss suffered by him in consequence of his resignation or the vacation of his benefice.[35] An incumbent found unable to perform the duties attaching to his benefice is entitled to his pension.

An incumbent may have one or more assistant curates, if he can get them and if the bishop is prepared to license them. An assistant curate must make the declaration of assent both before the bishop and, on the first Sunday on which he officiates, before the congregation at divine service. He must also take the oath of canonical obedience. Although an assistant curate's stipend was formerly payable by the incumbent himself, provision has now been made for payments by the Church Commissioners[36] towards such stipends. The incumbent can, with the bishop's permission, terminate the appointment by six months' notice; the assistant curate can terminate it by three months' notice; and, subject to appeal to the archbishop, the bishop can terminate it at any time.[37]

---

[35] See *In re Flenley*, [1981] Fam. 64, Compensation is in the first instance to be assessed by the Pastoral Committee of the diocese. The incumbent has a right of appeal to an Appeal Tribunal.

[36] Endowments and Globe Measure 1976 (No.4), s.8. see pp. 108 et seq.

[37] Canon C12 (5).

The incumbent must, either himself or by his assistants, provide his parishioners with the occasional offices of the Church (for example, baptism, marriage and burial), say Morning and Evening Prayer daily, preach at least one sermon each Sunday, and perform divine service on Sundays and holy days.[38]

The apportionment of England among parishes is very ancient, and the ancient apportionment and boundaries do not always accord with changing conditions. But no means exist for changing parish boundaries or for forming new parishes except by Act of Parliament or under statutory authority. There has, accordingly, in the last 150 years been a good deal of legislation to deal with this situation, most of which has now been codified in the Pastoral Measure 1983.[39] Provision now exists for carving new parishes out of one or more existing parishes, whereby the pastoral committee of the diocese may after obtaining the approval of the bishop submit draft proposals to the Church Commissioners who is turn may submit to the Queen in Council a draft pastoral scheme or order based on the proposals. Interested persons are given the opportunity of objecting to the scheme or order, and in the case of schemes (but not orders, which are less extensive[40]) objectors are allowed to seek leave to appeal to the Judicial Committee of the Privy Council. Clergy dispossessed by the implementation of a scheme are entitled to compensation.

A pastoral scheme may provide for the creation, dissolution or alteration of benefices or parishes, and deal with numerous ancillary matters. In particular, a scheme may depart from the traditional concept of allocating one incumbent to each parish, by establishing a team ministry or a group ministry. A team ministry involves the sharing of the cure of souls in the area of a benefice between a rector and one or more vicars, sometimes assisted by other persons authorized by licence or permission of the bishop. The team rector is presented or collated to the benefice, and may have a freehold office, or instead an office to be held for a term of years. He is a corporation sole and as such

38. Canon C24.
39. (No.1.) For a fuller account of this subject see Halsbury, vol. 14 paras. 856-891, and *A Handbook for Churchwardens and Parochial Church Councillors*, by Kenneth M. Macmorran (A.R. Mowbray & Co. Ltd.).
40. Pastoral Measure 1983 (No.1), s.37.

holds the property of the benefice during his term of office. It is
the rector who has the general responsibility for the cure of
souls, subject to any special cure or special responsibility of a
vicar. Each vicar in the team is normally appointed by licence
of the bishop, and holds his office for a specified term of years.
During that time he has security of tenure equivalent to that of
the incumbent of a benefice. Apart from any special functions
which may be assigned to him, a team vicar has (subject always
to the terms of his licence) authority to perform within the area
of the benefice all the offices and services of an incumbent. In
contrast to a team ministry, a group ministry involves the
extension of an incumbent's functions beyond his own benefice
to each of the other benefices in the group. Whilst performing
offices and services in a benefice in the group other than his
own, the incumbent has to act in accordance with the directions
of the incumbent of that benefice. He is not permitted during
the continuance of the group ministry to withdraw from the
duties of the group as a whole without resigning his own
benefice.

In the eighteenth century the Church suffered from two
closely linked scandals, absenteeism and pluralism. A cleric
who was well connected might acquire two or more benefices
which he would hold in plurality. He would himself pocket the
emoluments and pay less fortunately placed assistant curates a
pittance to do the work while he himself put in the minimum of
appearances. To deal with this scandal Parliament passed the
Pluralities Act, 1838,[41] and the Pluralities Act, 1850.[42] The
effect of this legislation is that, with certain exceptions, no one
may hold more than one benefice at a time. Thus the scandal
was scotched. But times changed and today the difficulty is to
find a sufficient number of clerics to man the parishes and
churches. What was required was provision to enable an
incumbent to look after two or more parishes and yet to guard
against a recrudescence of the former abuse. This was achieved
by the Pluralities Measure 1930.[43] the Union of Benefices
(Amendment) Measure, 1936,[44] and the Pastoral
Reorganisation Measure, 1949,[45] the joint effect being that
with leave an incumbent was able to hold the benefices in

[41]   1 & 2 Vict., c.106.   [44]   (No.2).
[42]   13 & 14 Vict., c.98.   [45]   (No.3).
[43]   (No.7).

plurality, or alternatively two or more parishes can be united. This body of legislation was replaced by the Pastoral Measure 1968[46] (itself repealed by the Pastoral Measure 1983[47]) but arrangements made under it remain valid until they are cancelled or spent.

There were three ways in which benefices might be held in plurality. The first was by dispensation from the Archbishop of Canterbury where the two churches were not more than four miles apart and the annual value of one of them did not exceed £400 a year.[48] The second was by the joint action of the bishop and the Church Commissioners and the Archbishop of Canterbury.[49] The third and simplest was by the bishop alone with the approval of the Church Commissioners.[50] There was usually included in the bishop's order a term precluding the incumbent from relinquishing one benefice unless he reliquished both. Sometimes it was provided that the incumbent should have specified help, either from assistant curates or from lay workers. Where, too, the patronage of the benefices was in different hands, provision had to be made for the exercise of the patronage by turns.

Union of benefices was effected under the Union of Benefices Measures, 1923 to 1952. In briefest outline, this was done by the Church Commissioners,[51] subject to an appeal by interested parties to the Privy Council.[52]

Where the benefices are held in plurality, the parishes remain distinct, but share a parson. When there has been a union of benefices, the old parishes will either be extinguished and a new parish formed out of their amalgamation, or the old parishes will still remain separate entities, whichever the scheme uniting them directs. But there can be only one parish church, and if more than one church remains in the united benefice, the scheme must direct which one is to be the parish church.

There remain to be noted only the guild churches of the City of London; but, since these are not really parish churches, they have been left to the next chapter.

[47.] (No.1).   [46.] (No.1).
[48.] Pluralities Act, 1838 (1 & 2 Vict., c.106), s.129, and Pluralities Measure, 1930, s.1.
[49.] Pluralities Measure, 1930 (No.7).
[50.] Pastoral Reorganization Measure, 1949 (No.3).   [51.] See pp. 108 et seq.
[52.] In the city of London, however, recourse had to be made to the Union of Benefices Act, 1860 (23 & 24 Vict., c.142), and the Union of Benefices Act, 1898 (61 & 62 Vict., c.23); see the Union of Benefices Measure, 1923 (No.2), s.45.

V

NON-PAROCHIAL UNITS

Although England is apportioned among a number of parishes, there are in addition some places which are not within a parish or even sometimes a diocese. These call for separate treatment, and a chapter to themselves.

1. CATHEDRALS

The most important of the non-parochial units are the cathedrals. It has been noted[1] that the cathedral is the church which has the bishop's *cathedra* or throne and that originally it was the only church of his *parochia* or diocese. One might, therefore, reasonably expect it to be the place of all places where the bishop was most at home; but, as matters have developed, it has become in fact in large measure independent of the bishop whose rights therein are more limited than in most of the churches in the diocese, although his throne is still in the cathedral.

Cathedrals fall into three main categories, namely (1) cathedrals of the old foundation, (2) cathedrals of the new foundation, and (3) parish church cathedrals.

The cathedrals of the old foundation are the ones which, before the Reformation, were secular[2] cathedrals, governed by a college of secular priests, such as York Minster, St. Paul's Cathedral, and Lincoln. The cathedrals of the new foundation are those which, before the Reformation, though cathedrals, were monastic, such as Canterbury and Winchester and Durham. To these of the new foundation may be added those, like Gloucester, which were not cathedrals before the Reformation, but which Henry VIII established as such after the Reformation along the same lines as he laid down for those cathedrals which had been monastic.

[1.] See p. 21 *ante*.
[2.] Secular clergymen are those who, unlike monks and friars, do not belong to a religious order imposing the threefold vow of poverty, chastity, and obedience.

In broad outline the constitutions of these two types of cathedral are similar; but one cannot generalize without great caution, for every cathedral is governed by its own constitution and statutes and there are many points of minor difference even between the cathedrals of the same type of foundation.

Each of these cathedrals of the new and of the old foundations has a dean and a chapter, the latter consisting of residentiary canons, usually about four in number. There is also a greater chapter, consisting of the dean and the residentiary canons and a number of honorary canons, usually about twenty. The dean is appointed by the Crown. In some cathedrals the residentiary canons are appointed by the Crown; but in most they are appointed by the bishop.[3] But sometimes the canonries are tied canonries; for example, at Ely one of the canonries was tied to the Ely Professorship in the University of Cambridge, and whoever was elected to that chair was automatically the holder of that canonry, while in Gloucester until recently one of the canonries was tied to the mastership of Pembroke College, Oxford. The honorary canons are appointed by the bishop, often as a mark of recognition for services rendered to the Church. Originally residentiary canons were called prebendaries, because their emoluments came from endowments known as prebends (from praebenda, pension); but, by the Ecclesiastical Commissioners Act, 1840,[4] they are to be styled *canons*; and the only persons today who are known as prebendaries are, ironically, the honorary canons is some cathedrals, who are not in receipt of any prebend at all.

The greater chapter (by whatever name it is called, and nomenclature varies from cathedral to cathedral) seldom has any function of importance to perform.[5] It elects the bishop; but since it has no choice as to who is to be elected,[6] this function cannot rank as important. It may also be summoned to advise the bishop, should he so wish. It is not uncommon for an

---

3. Most deans and residentiary canons are bound by the provisions of the Ecclesiastical Offices (Age Limit) Measure 1975 (No.2); see p. 42 *ante*.
4. 3 & 4 Vict., c.113. By this Act, deans and canons, other than professorial or honorary canons, must have been for at least six years in priest's orders.
5. York Minster differs from other cathedrals in that the administrative chapter consists of the dean, the residentiary canons, and some honorary canons, and is only the agent for the whole body of canons, residentiary and honorary.
6. See p. 20 *ante*.

honorary canon to deputize occasionally for a residentiary canon at a service in the cathedral.

The cathedral, subject to its constitution and statutes, is governed by the dean and the residentiary canons, commonly called the dean and chapter. The dean is the chairman of this body and takes the place of dignity in the cathedral next after the bishop. The bishop's rights in the cathedral are set out in the statutes, which specify the occasions when and the conditions under which he can of right preach and hold services and claim the assistance of the staff of the cathedral. Whereas the bishop is the ordinary of the rest of the diocese, he is not the ordinary of the cathedral. This means that the cathedral is not subject to the jurisdiction of the Consistory Court[7] of the diocese or to any archdeacon, and it does not require a faculty for anything which it does. This does not mean, as is sometimes thought, that a cathedral is above the law. It means merely that the process by which its actions are controlled by law is different from the normal process. The bishop is Visitor of the cathedral and at a visitation, if he finds that something has been done illegally, he can order that it be rectified. But he can probably no longer inflict ecclesiastical censures (or penalties) on individuals, as other provision has now been made for this,[8] bringing the clergy of the cathedrals under the same jurisdictions for purposes of discipline as those in the rest of the country.

It is uncertain whether the dean or the canons have cures of souls; but it is sometimes claimed that the dean has the cure of his chapter. Both have to reside in the precincts for a given number of days in the year, and each canon has further to take a period of close residence in the year, during which he is, as it were, the duty-canon.

There has from time to time been much legislation affecting the cathedrals; but most of it is now to be found in the Cathedrals Measure, 1963,[9] under which it is the duty of a Commission to provide new constitutions and statutes for each cathedral. These have to be laid before the General Synod and, if not rejected there, submitted to the Queen for implementation by an Order in Council. Among the provisions

7. See Chapter XIV *post*.
8. Ecclesiastical Jurisdiction Measure, 1963 (No.1); see Chapter XIV *post*.
9. No.2.

for each cathedral under the Measure is one providing that two of the residentiary canons shall be engaged exclusively on the business of the cathedral and that they and the dean shall be paid by the Church Commissioners. The reasons for this provision are two-fold. In the nineteenth century the property of the cathedrals was by statute expropriated and taken over by the Ecclesiastical Commissioners[10] (now the Church Commissioners) who, out of it, paid a fixed amount to the cathedrals and held the rest on trust for other pastoral purposes. With inflation, the amount fixed for each cathedral has become quite inadequate, and the Measure is in effect merely empowering the Commissioners to pay to the cathedrals a part of what orginally belonged to them. Added to this is the fact that of comparatively recent years such meagre emoluments as did attach to cathedral offices proved a temptation to bishops too strong to be resisted, and they adopted the device of subsidizing diocesan offices by making their holders canons, with the result that their work in the diocese was supported or augmented by their emoluments as canons, and their work as canons was seriously impeded by their diocesan commitments. This can still occur, with at times advantage to the cathedral as well as to the diocese, for it can be of benefit to both that a suffragan bishop or an archdeacon, for example, should also have a voice in the running of the mother-church of the diocese; but it can no longer occur in the case of the two canons who are to be supported financially by the Church Commissioners and are to be engaged exclusively on cathedral duties.

There are usually anything from one to four minor canons in each cathedral. They are sometimes known as priest vicars and sometimes as vicars choral, and they are not beneficed. In cathedrals of the new foundation one of them is usually precentor and the other sacrist (in cathedrals of the old foundation one of the canons is called precentor; but it is normal for a minor canon to be engaged to do the same work as a precentor in a cathedral of the new foundation). The precentor, in (sometimes strained) co-operation with the organist, looks after the music in the cathedral church, and the sacrist looks

---

[10]   See the Ecclesiastical Commissioners Act, 1836 (6 & 7 Will. IV, c.77), and the Ecclesiastical Commissioners Act, 1840 (3 & 4 Vict., c.113), and Chapter XI *post*.

after the vergers and furnishings, both as a rule working closely under the dean. In addition to the minor canons, there is usually employed in and about the cathedral a little army of persons—the organist, lay clerks (for singing), choristers, vergers, porters and builders and craftsmen, while the chapter is assisted by a chapter clerk, who is often a solicitor. There is also a registrar, who is a solicitor and often is also chapter clerk, and who has the task of registering such matters as the appointment of persons to freeholds in the cathedral. By the Measure there has also to be an architect. How many of these are under the visitatorial jurisdiction of the bishop and to what extent is a matter of some doubt and depends in part in each cathedral on its statutes. Though probably all of them are under an obligation to assist with information and to pay regard to monitions at visitations, none of them can be disciplined except by more normal process of law, when the fact that they had or had not paid heed to a monition at a visitation might be relevant to the propriety or otherwise of their conduct.

The parish church cathedrals are the creatures of modern legislation. On the creation of new dioceses it has often happened that a big parish church has been chosen as the cathedral, and the incumbent has found himself both parish priest and head of the new cathedral with the title of provost and with canons to assist him in the work of the cathedral and assistant curates to assist him in the work of the parish. The constitution and statutes of these cathedrals are complicated and have to provide for the dual role of the church both as the cathedral church of the diocese and also as the parish church of the district in which the parishioners have an interest.

In nearly every case the bishop is the patron of the benefice, and, therefore, the provost is appointed by him by way of collation,[11] and the canonries are either in the gift of the Crown or of the bishop. The parish church cathedral is placed outside the normal diocesan jurisdiction of the Consistory Court and of the archdeacon, though the archdeacons are members of the chapter. Provision is made for a large lay representation on the governing body of the cathedral and for the transfer to this body of the functions of the Parochial Church Council.[12] Provision is

[11.]   See p. 41. The provost is bound by the provisions of the Ecclesiastical Offices (Age Limit) Measure 1975 (No. 2); see p. 42 *ante*.
[12.]   See pp.37 et seq.

also made for the possibility of establishing a body of lay canons and defining their functions. (Although this provision is not confined by law to parish church cathedrals, it would seem probable that its implementation is more likely in such cathedrals.) Schemes prepared by the Cathedrals Commission may also make provision for a parish church cathedral to become a dean and chapter cathedral; but this may be done only with the consent of the Crown and of the patron, if the patron is not the bishop.[13]

Provision[14] is made for the removal of dignitaries for mental or physical incapacity. The expression includes deans, canons, prebendaries, archdeacons, and clergymen holding any freehold office other than the incumbents of parishes or members of royal peculiars. If the bishop thinks that a dignitary is thus incapacitated he must refer the matter to the greater chapter, which must afford an opportunity to the dignitary and to the bishop's representative to state their respective cases. It requires a two-thirds majority of those present and voting before it can be decided that the dignitary should retire. If the chapter does so decide by the necessary majority, the bishop may declare the office vacated or, if the office is in the appointment of the Crown, may petition the Queen, who may then declare the office vacated.

It remains to be noted that Christ Church, Oxford, is unique, being both a cathedral and an Oxford college. The Dean is head of both, and four of the six canons are also professors, and its constitution is peculiar to itself. The Church Dignitaries (Retirement) Measure[15] does not apply to Christ Church.

2. ROYAL PECULIARS

In some respects the two royal peculiars of Westminster Abbey and St. George's, Windsor, resemble cathedrals. They are not cathedrals, for they contain no bishop's throne. They are like cathedrals in that each is governed by a dean and chapter; but there the similarity ends, for they are entirely free both of episcopal and archiepiscopal jurisdiction. In this respect they are theological anomalies, for they are outside the episcopal

---

13. For all these matters see the Cathedrals Measure, 1963 (No.2).
14. Church Dignitaries (Retirement) Measure, 1949 (No.1).
15. Ibid.

stream. The dean in each case is the ordinary. The only, though considerable, check on their independence is that the Crown appoints the dean and the canons and is in each case the Visitor, and, as such, exercises the same sort of jurisdiction (through the Lord Chancellor) as the bishop exercises over his cathedral.

There are other royal peculiars, such as the chapels in the royal residences, and they too are subject only to the Crown.

3. OTHER PECULIARS

At one time there were some 300 peculiars in England, of which a few still survive.[16] They are like the royal peculiars in that they are free from the episcopal jurisdiction; they differ from the royal peculiars in that they are thought to be subject to the visitatorial jurisdiction of the Archbishop of Canterbury.

It is impossible to do more here than to note the existence of these peculiars, the more particularly since, in some cases, their status as peculiars has been challenged and the arrangements have not as yet been resolved. Bocking is probably a peculiar with a dean, but no canons. Battle's position as a peculiar has recently been challenged; like Bocking, however, it has a dean, but no canons. For many years it was thought that St. Edward's, Cambridge, was a peculiar. It is certainly an oddity; it is a parish in the middle of Cambridge with a chaplain appointed for a term of years by the Governing Body of Trinity Hall, and for many years the Bishop of Ely and the Chancellor and the Archdeacon claimed no authority over it, until one day someone stumbled upon an Order in Council of 1852 abolishing all peculiars in the geographical area of Ely (save for the Colleges). The Temple Church, Lincoln's Inn Chapel and Gray's Inn Chapel appear to be peculiars with, presumably, the Benchers of the respective Inns as the ordinary.

4. COLLEGE CHAPELS

Though they are not usually called peculiars, the colleges in the two Universities of Oxford and Cambridge claim to be outside

---

[16] Most having been abolished by the Ecclesiastical Commissioners Acts of 1836 (6 & 7 Will. IV, c.77) and 1850 (13 & 14 Vict., c.94).

the jurisdiction of the Bishops of Oxford and Ely respectively and to have each its own ordinary, usually the Governing Body of the college. In the case of the older colleges the claim might with difficulty be substantiated along the lines of the fiction of the lost grant. With the more modern colleges this line of argument would become even more difficult. There is, however, no doubt that in practice the colleges behave as though they are extra- diocesan, and their claim does not appear ever to have been overtly contested. Nor is it in any way clear whether the ordinary is, in respect of the chapel, visitable by the Visitor of the college, the Archbishop of Canterbury, or both, or neither.

5. PRIVATE CHAPELS

At one time it was common for the owner of a great house to provide a private chapel for himself and his household and to appoint a chaplain. This can still occur, but the interests of the parish and of its incumbent have to be respected. The chaplain, like any other priest, requires a licence or written permission to officiate from the bishop, who has complete discretion to refuse it; and, even if the bishop is willing to grant such a licence, the incumbent's consent is also necessary.[17] Canon B41 furthermore provides that the Holy Communion shall be administered in such private chapels only 'seldom upon Sunday and other greater Feast Days, so that the residents in the said house may resort to their parish church and there attend divine service'.

Where a number of persons joined together to provide themselves with a place of worship, the building came to be known as a proprietary chapel; but a proprietary chapel is in law no different from any other private chapel, and the rights of the incumbent of the parish are the same.

Indeed, the incumbent's rights in his own parish are such that in strict law it would be possible for an incumbent to refuse to allow the ministrations which today are often provided by chaplains in large holiday camps catering for several thousand different persons in each week, and this situation can be altered only by legislation.

[17.] *Jones* v. *Jelf*, [1863] 8 L.T. 399. Canon C8.

6. OTHER EXCEPTIONS

Legislation has in fact been passed to remove from incumbents their jurisdiction in respect of various institutions.

Public schools, prisons, cemeteries, and hospitals all have their own chaplains and places of worship, and statutory provision has in each case been made to enable this to come about.[18] The chaplain requires the licence of the bishop but not the consent of the incumbent, and the chaplain decides on the disposal of moneys collected at the services, but subject to the direction of the bishop.[19]

The Armed Forces of the Crown also appear to provide exceptions. The position of the chaplains would seem to rest on the royal prerogative rather than on statute, for, in the main, they are regulated by Queen's Regulations, Admiralty Instructions, and Air Council Instructions.[20]

In the Royal Navy the Chaplain of the Fleet is the chief chaplain. In the Army the chaplains (of all denominations other than Roman Catholic) are under the Chaplain-General to the Forces, and in the Royal Air Force they are under the Chaplain-in-Chief. Rather suprisingly, in the first instance at the instigation of King Edward VII, each of the chief chaplains is styled *archdeacon*.[21]

In so far as they are not bound by their respective Service regulations, the chaplains to the Forces (of the Church of England) are under the Archbishop of Canterbury, who exercises supervision over them through, at the moment, the Bishop Suffragan of Croydon.

7. GUILD CHURCHES

The City of London provides exceptions to many things, and included among the exceptions are its so-called guild churches. They were created as such by the City of London (Guild Churches) Act, 1952,[22] advantage being taken of the necessary

18. Public Schools Act, 1868 (31 & 32 Vict., c.118); Endowed Schools Act, 1869 (32 & 33 Vict., c.56); Prison Act, 1952 (15 & 16 Geo. VI and I Eliz. II, c.52); Cemetery Clauses Act, 1847 (10 & 11 Vict., c.65); National Health Service Act, 1946 (9 & 10 Geo. VI, c.81).
19. Private Chapels Act, 1871 (34 & 35 Vict., c.66)
20. But see also Army Chaplains Act, 1868 (31 & 32 Vict., c.83).
21. According to Archbishop Fisher, because they are his 'oculi'.
22. 15 & 16 Geo. VI and I Eliz. II, c.xxxviii.

reorganization as a result of war damage to remedy a situation brought about initially by the large number of parish churches in the City which had formerly catered for a very small resident population and were really redundant, but which, by reason of their architectural merit and antiquity, called for preservation.

Sixteen of these churches have been designated *guild churches* (for lack of any better name). They have ceased to be ordinary parish churches, and their former territory has been allocated to neighbouring parishes. The guild churches are themselves free of the jurisdiction of the incumbents of the enlarged parishes in which they now find themselves geographically situated. Each has its own incumbent called the guild vicar, who is presented by the patron to the bishop and who is appointed for a term of years. Each also has its churchwardens, a Guild Church Council and an electoral roll of persons who apply to be put upon it (without prejudice to any other roll on which they may be) and who declare that they are over sixteen, members of the Church of England, and not members of any religious body not in communion with the Church of England. Each guild church is supposed to have its own specialty, and each guild vicar is also supposed to have his own personal specialty. Every guild church also tries to make provision for the spiritual needs of the weekday workers in the City and for the many tourists who come there. A guild church seldom functions on Saturdays, or Sundays, or great festivals such as Easter or Christmas, since at such times the City is virtually deserted.

VI

DOCTRINE

So far we have been considering the constitutional structure of the Church, and there is still more in this respect with which it will be necessary to deal later. A structure should serve some useful purpose, and the question might well be asked: for what purpose has this complicated structure been erected?

The Church claims to be the Body of Christ,[1] and as such charged to continue on earth the ministry of her incarnate Lord, the Lord who said,[2] 'My meat is to do the will of him that sent me, and to finish his work'; and who charged his disciples to go into all the world, and preach the gospel to every living creature,[3] and added, 'He that believeth and is baptised shall be saved. . . . In my name they shall cast out devils . . . they shall lay hands on the sick, and they shall recover', who taught and prayed, and who took bread and blessed and brake and gave it and also wine and said, 'This do in remembrance of me.'[4] In obedience to her Lord's commands and after his example the Church's main work may conveniently be divided into teaching and worshipping, including therein the ministry of the word and sacraments. This is not to ignore works of charity and mercy, incumbent upon all Christians individually; but it is with the corporate work of the Church with which we are immediately concerned, for it is corporate activities which require to be regulated by laws.

Doctrine and worship are, of course, closely linked. Doctrine determines liturgy and a study of liturgy reveals doctrine. Not much, however, will be said in this chapter about doctrine. It is fundamental to the whole law of the Church; but its detailed exposition must be sought in works devoted to that subject. No more will appear in this chapter than is necessary for an understanding of the law.

[1.] See, e.g., 1 Corinthians xii. 27; Ephesians i. 23; and Colossians i. 18.
[2.] John iv. 34.
[3.] Mark xvi. 15 et seq.
[4.] 1 Corinthians xi. 23-26.

The doctrine of the Church of England, like its canon law, is that of the Western Catholic Church immediately before the Reformation, but subject to the modifications introduced by the Reformation, sometimes explicitly and sometimes implicitly. Recourse must, therefore, be had to the Book of Common Prayer, the Thirty-nine Articles, the Canons of 1603, and the Homilies; to Acts of Parliament and to the judgments of the courts. All these in varying degrees may be said to be authoritative—not necessarily right, but binding until altered. Article XIX says, 'As the Church of *Jerusalem*, *Alexandria*, and *Antioch*, have erred; so also the Church of *Rome* has erred'; and honesty will compel us to add, 'So also, just conceivably, might the Church of England err.' To Bishop Rawlinson of Derby is attributed the *bon mot*, 'The Church of Rome claims to be infallible. The Church of England is more modest in her claims; she merely says that she is right.' It should be noted, too, that the courts do not claim to declare true doctrine, but only to state what the law is with regard to doctrine. 'This Court has no jurisdiction or authority to settle matters of faith', said the Privy Council, 'or to determine what ought in any case to be the doctrine of the Church of England. Its duty extends only to a consideration of that which is by law established to be the doctrine of the Church of England upon the true and legal construction of the articles and formularies.'[5] In addition to these authoritative sources, there are others of considerable persuasive authority, such as the resolutions of Lambeth Conferences, acts of Convocation,[6] and reports of Commissions, in particular the report on *Doctrine in the Church of England*.[7] This last is especially valuable in that it indicates the differences of view which are held and which are allowable within the Church of England.

A word of caution, too, is needed before recourse is made to post-Reformation sources which have been termed authoritative. As has been remarked before,[8] when dealing with the Book of Common Prayer it must be remembered that,

---

[5] *Gorham* v. *Bishop of Exeter*, [1850] Moore's Special Report, 462.
[6] See p.27 *ante*.
[7] The Report of the Commission on Christian Doctrine appointed by the Archbishops of Canterbury and York in 1922 (SPCK).
[8] See p. 8 *ante*.

although it has statutory authority, it is not itself an Act of Parliament and should not be construed as such. Its rubrics, though binding, are clerical directives, written in the seventeenth century by clerics for the guidance largely of clerics, and unless they are interpreted as such, and in the context of the seventeenth century, they will not make sense.[9] They must be interpreted with the elasticity which directives usually require. On the other hand, the Thirty-nine Articles require the strictest literal interpretation. It is essential to remember that they must be read together with His Majesty's Declaration, which forms the Preface to them[10] and which states explicitly, '. . . no man hereafter shall either print, or preach, to draw the Article aside in any way, but shall submit to it in the plain and full meaning thereof: and shall not put his own sense or comment to be the meaning of the Article, but shall take it in the literal and grammatical sense'. So taken, many points in the Articles which on a superficial reading cause difficulty and offence will be seen to be innocuous.

In any event, England has never proved the happiest hunting- ground for heresy-hunters. In matters of doctrine an enormous measure of liberty in interpretation especially of recent years has in practice been allowed (and the Church of England has often been criticized for this); and a considerable measure of liberty is permitted by the law.[11] Certainly with the post-Reformation formularies, where two interpretations are possible, either will be permitted; and with regard to matters on which post-Reformation formularies are silent, Article VI expressly states that 'Holy Scripture containeth all things necessary to salvation: so that whatsoever is not read therein, nor may be proved thereby, is not to be required of any man, that it should be believed as an article of the Faith, or be thought requisite or necessary to salvation.' The very toleration which the Church here displays has at times provided the opportunity to some of her members, not only to air their own unusual views on matters of faith, but also to seek to include therein, as though

[9] See *Bishopwearmouth (Rector and Churchwardens)* v. *Adey (1958)*, 3 All E.R. 441 at p.444.
[10] Ibid. See also *Gorham* v. *Bishop of Exeter, supra.*
[11] *Gorham* v. *Bishop of Exeter, supra*, P.C. *H.M. Procurator-General* v. *Stone,* [1808] 1 Hag. Con. 424, at p. 429; *Sheppard* v. *Bennett (2nd Appeal),* [1871] L.R. 4 P.C. 371, at p. 418; *Williams* v. *Salisbury (Bishop),* [1863] 2 Moo. P.C. (n.s.) 375.

necessary to salvation, their views on a variety of matters of social policy, ranging through such divers subjects as the welfare state, the nuclear deterrent, and prohibition, in respect of which it might be thought very difficult to find supporting proof in Holy Scripture. Such is the tenderness displayed today towards the claims of conscience that the Ecclesiastical Jurisdiction Measure 1963,[12] expressly states that proceedings for unbecoming conduct are not to be taken against a clergyman in respect of his political opinions, thus leaving wide open the door to all sorts of unedifying eccentricities. But, nevertheless, there are degrees of heterodoxy which provide a breaking-point for the toleration even of the English and of their law. In the case of the clergy these are more often revealed in matters of public worship than in matters of public teaching, for English pragmatism seems often more concerned with what a man does than with what he says or thinks, and, in the conduct of public worship, pragmatism is reinforced by a conservatism which is quick to resent innovations in divine worship while remaining tolerant of innovations in the exposition of doctrine. Some of these instances will be noted later.

It is not only with the clergy, however, that the law is concerned. The conduct of the laity in matters of orthodoxy is also cognizable by the courts, and by the secular courts at that. It required a number of statutes to relieve from disabilities those whose consciences precluded them from conforming to the Church of England, the most noteworthy of them being the Toleration Act, 1688,[13] the Nonconformist Relief Act, 1779,[14] the Promissory Oaths Acts, 1868 and 1871,[15] the Endowed Schools Act, 1869,[16] and the Universities Tests Act, 1871.[17] As a result, it may fairly be said that no legal disabilities now attach to nonconformity, while in the Education Acts, 1944 and 1946,[18] Parliament has almost tumbled over backwards to preserve the rights of parents with regard to the religious education of their children, even going so far as to provide that religious instruction and the collective worship with which the day is to begin may not be distinctive of any particular religious

---

[12.] (No. 1), s.14.
[13.] 1 Will. and Mar., c.18.   [14.] 19 Geo. III, c.44.
[15.] 31 & 32 Vict., c.72, and 34 & 35 Vict., c.48.   [16.] 32 & 33 Vict., c.56.
[17.] 34 & 35 Vict., c.26.   [18.] 7 & 8 Geo. VI, c. 31 and 9 & 10 Geo. VI, c.50.

denominations—provisions which it might reasonably be argued are contradictions in terms, at any rate so far as worship is concerned. Furthermore, Nonconformist ministers, while enjoying all the freedom of laymen, also share some of the privileges of clerks in holy orders, being free from jury service (and, in the days when for others it was compulsory, from the obligations to serve as churchwardens),[19] and being afforded special protection under the Offences against the Persons Act, 1861.[20] Roman Catholics, too, are now by statute free from most disabilities.[21] No Roman Catholic, however, may be on the throne, nor may the Sovereign's Consort be a Roman Catholic.[22] Statute now provides that the Lord Chancellor may be a Roman Catholic.[23] Roman Catholics, too, are barred from holding ecclesiastical office, and so a Roman Catholic cannot be chancellor of a diocese.[24] If he is the patron of a benefice, he has an empty privilege, for the right of presentation is exercised by one of the two ancient universities.[25] Although no prohibition is placed upon a Roman Catholic's being a Minister of the Crown, he may not advise with regard to any office in the Church.[26]

Roman Catholic priests share with Nonconformist ministers exemption from jury service,[27] and with Anglican priests they are disqualified from sitting in the House of Commons.[28] By the Ecclesiastical Titles Act, 1871,[29] no one may assume the title of archbishop, bishop, or dean of any place, if that title is already appropriated to the Church of England—a statutory

---

19. See the legislation already cited and the Juries Act, 1974 (22 & 23 Eliz. II, c.23)
20. 24 & 25 Vict., c.100, s.36.
21. See the legislation already cited, Roman Catholic Relief Act, 1791 (31 Geo. III, c.32), and the Roman Catholic Relief Act, 1829 (10 Geo. IV, c.7).
22. Bill of Rights, 1688 (1 Will. and Mar., Seps. 2 c.2), and Act of Settlement, 1700 (12 & 13 Will. III, c.2); Roman Catholic Relief Act, 1829 (supra), s.16.
23. Lord Chancellor (Tenure of Office and Discharge of Ecclesiastical Functions) Act 1974 (22 & 23 Eliz.II, c.25).
24. Roman Catholic Relief Act, 1829 supra, s16.
25. Presentation of Benefices Acts, 1605 (3 Jas. I, c.5), 1688 (1 Will. and Mar. c.26), and 1713 (13 Anne, c.13).
26. Roman Catholic Relief Act, 1829, supra.
27. Roman Catholic Relief Act, 1791, and Juries Act 1974, supra.
28. Roman Catholic Relief Act, 1829, supra, and House of Commons (Clergy Disqualification) Act, 1801 (41 Geo. III, c. 63), and see p. 126 post.
29. 34 & 35 Vict., c.53.

provision aimed primarily at Roman Catholics.

Despite this substantial measure of toleration, and the repeal of a number of ancient statutes designed to protect the Christian religion, some legal restrictions still survive. It is a common law offence to scoff at or impugn the Christian faith or the Holy Scriptures or the person of Our Lord.[30] It would, however, seem that it is at least not the policy of the secular law to suppress the sober and decent expression of views which cannot be reconciled with orthodox doctrine[31], and persons with no religious beliefs and Unitarians, Jews, Muslims, and others not only are left completely free to follow their own devices, but even receive statutory assistance[32] which would seem to be inconsistent with its being an offence merely to maintain arguments against the Christian religion. The truth is that this is a part of the law which is encrusted with the remnants of ancient controversies and struggles, as much political as religious, and that, pending an exhaustive revision, it has been swept into a corner where for most of the time it lies conveniently forgotten. One never knows, however, when a breeze may not suddenly arise and blow the dust out of the corner. The time may well be ripe for the passing of an Act designed to protect religious susceptibilities of all sorts from vulgar abuse while leaving the field open to serious argument and discussion.

It need scarcely be said that whatever is in a layman a secular offence against doctrine is also a secular offence in a clergyman. These secular offences, and more besides, are probably still ecclesiastical offences in a layman, formerly cognizable in the ecclesiastical courts with the sanction of ecclesiastical censure; but the use of the ecclesiastical courts for the trial of laymen for doctrinal offences has long since ceased, and no provision for their trial is contained in the Ecclesiastical Jurisdiction Measure, 1963.[33]

With the clergy, however, it is different. It is reasonable to

---

30.   *R* v. *Lemon* (1979) 1 All E.R. 898
31.   *Bowman* v. *Secular Society, Ltd.* (1917), A.C. 406; *R. v. Ramsay and Foote.* [1883] 48 L.T. 733; *R. v. Boulter* (1908), 72 J.P. 188.
32.   e.g. the registration of synagogues under the Places of Worship Registration Act, 1855 (18 & 19 Vict., c.81).
33.   (No. 1.)

require of the officers of any organization a degree of orthodoxy which it might not be reasonable to require of others. Ecclesiastical censures, moreover, involving possibly deprivation and unfrocking, can be of practical value to the Church and a measure of deterrence to clerks. It would, therefore, be wrong to suppose that proceedings in the ecclesiastical courts for doctrinal offences are a thing of the past, and the elaborate provisions in the Ecclesiastical Jurisdiction Measure, 1963, for dealing with such cases are an indication that the jurisdiction is very much alive. It is, however, still true to say that a large measure of toleration is extended both in practice and by the law. But the teaching of false doctrine by a clerk in holy orders is undoubtedly an offence, provided it can be shown that what has been taught is directly contrary to the doctrines of the Church of England and is not on one of those points upon which no declaration has, expressly or by implication, been authoritatively made.

But, as has been observed, doctrinal offences are more likely to obtrude themselves in connexion with some other matter, more particularly in connexion with ceremonial, than as pure points of doctrine, and we shall notice these as we come to them.

VII

WORSHIP

Among Church folk forms of public worship provide perhaps the most fruitful source of dissension. To those outside the Church this seems meaningless and trivial. So it very often is. But the gibes directed at the Church in this respect are by no means wholly justified. The ceremonial used in a service can be as important as the words. Words express thought in sound, and gestures express it in action. Doctrine is imbedded in liturgy and liturgy declares doctrine. Much of the controversy about rites and ceremonies[1] is a controversy between conservatism and innovation, and both are often misconceived. Much of it is aesthetic, yet aesthetics can be very important. But much of it is at root doctrinal and expresses theological differences, often profound, but not necessarily irreconcilable, though to the protagonists at any given moment they may appear so.

The long-drawn-out period of the Reformation was, of course, a period of controversy, political and theological. The architects of the Reformation settlement sought to inculcate unity by imposing uniformity, partly because theological unity was a source of political strength,[2] and partly because they realized more acutely than perhaps we do today that, when faith is lively, it dictates the works which result. Bigotry, of course, at times had ample scope. But bitter experience begat a measure of wisdom, and by the middle of the seventeenth century in their search for unity they had learnt to try to be irenic. The Act of Uniformity, 1662,[3] imposed on the nation a Prayer Book from which none might deviate. It was hoped that its use would make all like-minded only are left outward conformity would not merely reflect, but would actually create, unanimity. Though

[1] These words are often misused even by dictionaries. Strictly, a *rite* is a form of words. A *ceremony* is a form of action. See *The Oxford Dictionary of the Christian Church*, p.258 (ceremonial) and p.1168 (ritual); also Halsbury, vol.14 para.953.

[2] Cf. the preamble to the Act of Uniformity, 1662 (14 Car. II, c.4).

[3] 14 Car. II, c.4.

this has not been achieved, the attempt has had a surprising measure of success. This, in part at least, is due to the fact that its framers placed as little strain as they felt able upon the consciences of individuals. Where it was possible to do so, the language employed was such as to tempt the cynic to say that it does not commit anyone to either a Catholic or a Protestant interpretation; but, in truth, it is such as to include both. In the Order for the Administration of the Lord's Supper, for example, both the sacrificial and the merely commemorative elements are present. The minister is called a priest, which implies sacrifice, while the board is called a table and not an altar, thereby suggesting a different implication. It was no doubt hoped that this careful construction of the Book would make it more easily palatable over a wide range of theological taste. In this respect success has largely been achieved. Though the Book probably satisfies no one wholly (and no book would do that), it has won the affection of many and the toleration of most.

The main difficulty has arisen by reason of the attempt to give the Book a monopoly in the field of public worship and to allow no deviations from it. Both have proved impracticable. There are occasions for which the Book makes no adequate provision; and there are other occasions when the provision made by the Book is inappropriate to immediate needs. It is, then, no wonder that a situation has arisen in which it is probably true to say that there is not a single minister who uses the Book without some deviations from it and not a single church where the Book, the whole Book, and nothing but the Book, is used in the manner intended.

This is not to say that in every such instance the law has been broken. Strict as are the provisions aimed at securing complete uniformity, it is not every departure from the Book which is unlawful.[4]

The Act of Uniformity itself remembered that members of the royal family are not immortal and made provision for altering the prayers relating to them as occasion may require.[5]

Parliament permitted a very few very minor modifications by the Act of Uniformity Amendment Act, 1872,[6] and another

---

[4.]   Canon B5 permits variations 'which are not of substantial importance'.
[5.]   1662, s.21.

Act permits further modifications in the college chapels of Oxford, Cambridge, and Durham with the consent of the Visitor.[7]

A considerably wider power to introduce forms of service other than those contained in the Book is conferred upon the General Synod by the Church of England (Worship and Doctrine) Measure 1974[8] and Canon B2. It is now lawful for the General Synod to approve, amend, continue or discontinue any form of service; but its powers are limited in two important respects. The forms of service contained in the Book of Common Prayer must continue to be available for use, whatever alternative provision is made for worship; and any proposal under the Measure must be approved by a majority in each House of the General Synod of two-thirds of those present and voting.[9] Canon B3 governs the selection at parochial level from amongst the forms of service permitted by law. Decisions concerning services other than those known as occasional offices[10] are to be taken jointly by the minister and the parochial church council. In the event of disagreement, the services contained in the Book of Common Prayer are to be used, unless other authorised forms of service were in use in the church during at least two of the preceding four years and the parochial church council resolves that those other forms shall be used. It is, however for the minister to select the form of the occasional offices (other than the Order of Confirmation); but if a person concerned objects beforehand the matter must be referred to the bishop of the diocese.

Canon C15 lays down the declaration of assent which every priest and deacon has to make, and it is in the following terms:

I . . . declare my belief in the faith which is revealed in the Holy Scriptures and set forth in the catholic creeds and to which the historic formularies of the Church of England bear witness; and in public prayer and administration of the sacraments, I will use only the forms of service which are authorised or allowed by Canon.

[6.] 35 & 36 Vict., c.35.
[7.] The Universities Tests Act, 1871 (34 & 35 Vict., c.26).
[8.] No. 3.
[9.] The Alternative Service Book 1980 was introduced under this Measure.
[10.] Occasional offices are not defined but are generally accepted to be services other than those which are held regularly.

It is to be noted that it is to *public* prayer and to the administration of the sacraments that the declaration applies. These cover a very important and wide area; but they do not cover the whole area. In truly private services, other than the administration of the sacraments, the Prayer Book need not be followed.

It is also to be noted that the Prayer Book need not be followed if lawful authority decrees otherwise. The difficulty here, however, is that nobody knows what the term *lawful authority* comprises. Clearly an Act of Parliament or a Measure of the Church Assembly or General Synod is lawful authority. Is anybody or anything else lawful authority, and, if so, who or what?

Much ink has been spilt and many words poured forth in an attempt to discover the meaning of lawful authority, and it is now clear that the meaning is elusive and that no interpretation is likely to meet with general acceptance.[11] By far the most workable explanation is that provided by Mr. Justice Vaisey.[12] He suggests that lawful authority can be determined only by reference to the context of the occasion on which the deviation is made. Thus, at one end of the scale, the addition of prayers of thanksgiving by the whole nation for deliverance from some national catastrophe might be lawfully authorized by royal proclamation with the approval of the two archbishops; lower in the scale, prayers for the success of some diocesan venture might be lawfully authorized by the bishop of the diocese concerned; and, lower still, intercessions in respect of some sudden, local disaster (in, for example, a mining village) could be lawfully authorized by the parish priest. It is by no means universally accepted that the learned Judge's explanation is the right one, and it leaves open the question of which authority in any given situation is the appropriate one. But it has the merit of introducing just that element of elasticity without which a common prayer-book cannot meet the manifold unpredicted and unpredictable occasions for which provision is required.[13]

Closely linked with the problem of lawful authority is the

11. See *Rossi* v. *Edinburgh Corporation* (1905), A.C. 21.
12. "Lawful Authority', a Memorandum', to be found at pp. 215 et seq. of *The Canon Law of the Church of England*, being the Report of the Archbishops' Commission on Canon Law (SPCK 1947).
13. Canons B4 and B5 attempt to meet these difficulties by specifying the authority which can authorise forms of service for which no other provision is made.

doctrine of the *jus liturgicum*, which is part of pre-Reformation canon law, and according to which, in some circumstances, it lies with the bishop to authorize what would otherwise be unlawful. The doctrine finds a faint echo in that prefatory chapter to the Book of Common Prayer entitled 'Concerning the Service of the Church' where the following passage occurs:

And forasmuch as nothing can be so plainly set forth, but doubts may arise in the use and practice of the same; to appease all such diversity (if any arise) and for the resolution of all doubts, concerning the manner how to understand, do, and execute, the things contained in this Book; the parties that so doubt, or diversly take any thing, shall resort to the Bishop of the Diocese, who by his discretion shall take order for the quieting and appeasing of the same; so that the same order be not contrary to any thing contained in this Book. And if the Bishop of the Diocese be in doubt then he may send for the resolution thereof to the Archbishop.

It would seem that this reference to the bishop is limited to 'the manner how to understand, do, and execute, the things contained in this Book', whereas the *jus liturgicum*, while it might be taken to cover that ground, is concerned with a wider field than that which is contained in the Prayer Book.

It is submitted that there is no reason to suppose that the *jus liturgicum* has been abrogated by the Reformation settlement; but it has certainly been affected by it. It clearly would not lie with the bishop to authorize anything forbidden by the Book of Common Prayer, for the Book has statutory authority. Nor, for the same reason, could he authorize the omission of anything enjoined by the Book. But, over that wide area for which no provision is made one way or the other, it is submitted that the *jus liturgicum* can still operate, and, indeed, that the exigencies of a situation may demand that it *should* operate in order to supply what would otherwise be grievously wanting.[14] It would seem, however, that there can be no legal validity in the purported exercise of an alleged episcopal discretion to allow the wholesale use of the deposited Prayer Book of 1928 which the House of Commons rejected. Though this decision was taken in 1929 by all the bishops, however excusable (and possibly laudable) on other grounds such a decision may have been, it

14. See *Martin* v. *Mackonochie*, [1868] L.R. 2 A. & E. 116, and L.R. 2 P.C. 365. For a further discussion of the *jus liturgicum* and of the doctrine of necessity see Chapter VIII *post*, on the Holy Communion and in particular for a discussion of *Re Lapford* (1954), 3 All E.R. 484.

could neither bind the successors to the individual bishops nor operate in any case where provision had already been made by the lawful Book of 1662. It is, however, submitted that in respect of services for which the Book of 1662 made no provision, such as Prime and Compline, the authorization by a bishop of forms of service for use in his own diocese, whether taken from the Book of 1928 or from elsewhere, would be a legitimate exercise of the jus liturgicum.

There is yet one further legal doctrine which may at times be prayed in aid to justify departures from the Book of Common Prayer. It is the doctrine of necessity, known to all branches of the law of England, though about which there is singularly little authority. It is the doctrine which justifies the surgeon in committing what is *prima facie* a crime when, for the health of his patient, he plunges his knife into the abdomen in order to remove a troublesome appendix, or when, to save the life of the mother, he procures an abortion.[15] It is the doctrine which has resulted in there being no recorded case of a prosecution of a fireman for pulling down property in order to prevent the spread of fire. It is submitted that the doctrine applies equally to matters ecclesiastical. It is the only legal doctrine which, for example, would justify a priest in administering the Holy Communion to a person who by reason of infirmity was unable to kneel as directed by the rubric.[16] There would seem to be other instances when the doctrine of necessity may be invoked to justify a departure from the strict letter of the Book of Common Prayer. But great caution is required in the application of the doctrine. Before anyone can avail himself of it, he must show that the act, *prima facie* illegal, which he has committed, was the lesser of two evils and the only reasonable way of averting the greater evil. The evil averted must be greater than the evil committed, and no more may be done contrary to the legal prohibition or injunction than is at once necessary and reasonable to avert the greater evil.

Despite the relaxations which it is thought are provided by reliance on lawful authority, the *jus liturgicum*, and the doctrine of necessity, the Book of Common Prayer, with all its merits,

15. *R. v. Bourne* (1938), 3 All E.R. 615. See also pp. 74, 113 and 155 *post* and *Bishopwearmouth (Rector and Churchwardens) v. Adey* (1958), 3 All E.R. 441.

16. At the end of the Order for the Administration of the Lord's Supper. This and similar difficulties may now be overcome by relying on Canon B5.

has become a straitjacket, not merely restricting growth and experiment, but also preventing, if obeyed, the provision of appropriate worship on occasions never foreseen by the compilers of the Book. The result is that the Book is not obeyed. Faced with the alternative of being obedient at the cost of failing to provide for the hungry sheep, or of feeding the hungry sheep at the cost of disobedience, the pastors of the flocks have put first the duty of feeding the sheep, even though this may involve disobedience in minor particulars. It is an alternative which should never have been forced upon them, and no one can contemplate with equanimity a situation in which all are forced to connive at disobedience; for disobedience in small particulars begets an attitude of lawlessness which soon overflows into matters of moment and passes unchecked by an authority which itself is already compromised by its connivance in the minor matters. That such a state of affairs should continue to exist long after the inadequacies of the authorized book have become apparent is evidence of the existence within the Church of fairly deep-seated theological cleavages. Had it not been for these, agreed relaxations might well have received statutory authority. There are fissures in the fabric of the Establishment, and the wallpaper of uniformity no longer conceals the cracks, but is itself rent asunder by them. The task of revising the forms of public worship is slow and difficult because, in some measure at least, it is the task of resolving theological differences within the Church and of determining the limits of toleration for such different views as a single Church can permit without losing all force and direction. The Church of England (Worship and Doctrine) Measure 1974[17] and the Canons now provide some legal machinery for altering the forms of service, providing additional forms, and permitting variations in appropriate circumstances. It remains to be seen how far this legislation succeeds in alleviating the situation.

If he has never done so already, the reader is advised, next time he returns from church, to open his Prayer Book and read through the provisions for the service he has just attended and note how closely or otherwise the Book and the service agree. In the following chapters some aspects of these services are considered from the legal angle.

[17.] No. 3.

VIII

BAPTISM, CONFIRMATION, AND HOLY COMMUNION

The Catechism in the Book of Common Prayer defines a sacrament as 'an outward and visible sign of an inward and spiritual grace given unto us, ordained by Christ himself, as a means whereby we receive the same, and a pledge to assure us thereof'. While it is generally accepted that a sacrament is an outward and visible sign of an inward and spiritual grace, the term has not always been confined to those clearly ordained by Christ himself, and in the twelfth century it was suggested that there were as many as thirty sacraments.[1] Today seven is the most commonly accepted number, namely, Baptism, Confirmation, Holy Communion, Penance, Unction, Holy Orders, and Matrimony. But the Catechism, having first confined the term to those ordained by Christ himself, goes on to limit the number to 'two only, as generally necessary to salvation; that is to say, Baptism, and the Supper of the Lord', while the Thirty-nine Articles say that the other five, 'commonly called Sacraments . . . are not to be counted for Sacraments of the Gospel . . . for that they have not any visible sign of ceremony ordained of God'.[2]

The question of nomenclature is not important. If a sacrament is an outward and visible sign of an inward and spiritual grace, then there are more sacraments than two. If, however, the term is confined to those ordained by Christ himself, some further term is required for 'those commonly called Sacraments' (and others) which were either not ordained by Christ or about which, in this respect, there may be controversy. It is quite clear that the central act of worship of the Catholic Church, both in the East and in the West, finds its focus in the great sacrament of the Body and Blood of Christ,

---

[1] Hugh of St. Victor in his *De Sacramentis Christianae Fidei*.
[2] Emphasis here lies on the sign or ceremony, for the prayer in the marriage service speaks of matrimony as 'instituted of God in the time of man's innocency'.

sometimes known as the Eucharist, sometimes as the Mass, sometimes as the Lord's Supper, sometimes as the Liturgy, and sometimes as the Holy Communion. Upon it most other acts of worship hinge, or else they take place within its context. It would therefore, be appropriate to begin with a study of this sacrament, but for the fact that baptism is a condition precedent to the reception of Holy Communion, and confirmation is normally a condition precedent. It is, therefore, convenient to consider all three together, beginning with baptism and confirmation.

Baptism is the means whereby a person is admitted into the Church. Over the centuries there has been considerable speculation and controversy about its precise theological significance, to all of which the Church of England sits somewhat lightly and is not swift to condemn any view, provided it is not inconsistent with the little that is stated in the Book of Common Prayer and the Thirty-nine Articles.[3] According to Article XXVII:

Baptism is not only a sign of profession, and mark of difference, whereby Christian men are discerned from others that be not christened, but it is also a sign of Regeneration or new Birth, whereby, as by an instrument, they that receive baptism rightly are grafted into the Church; the promises of forgiveness of sin, and of our adoption to be the sons of God by the Holy Ghost, are visibly signed and sealed; Faith is confirmed, and Grace increased by virtue of prayer unto God.

According to the Catechism, it is 'a death unto sin, and a new birth unto righteousness: for being by nature born into sin, and the children of wrath, we are hereby made the children of grace'.

The means whereby baptism is effected is by immersing the candidate in water, or pouring water upon him, in the name of the Father and of the Son and of the Holy Ghost; and that is all that is essential.[4] While the Prayer Book clearly contemplates that it shall be administered by the parish priest in church, it may be administered anywhere at any time by anybody, even, it is said, by an unbeliever; and the Ordinal expressly states that 'it appertaineth to the office of a Deacon ... in the absence of the Priest to baptize infants'. In the case of those who are of riper

3. *Gorham v. Bishop of Exeter* [1850] Moore's Special Reports, 462.
4. See Canon B25; and also Canon 30 of 1603, though repealed.

years, the Prayer Book and Canon B24 direct that notice of a proposed baptism should be given beforehand to the bishop,[5] though, no doubt, in a case of urgency it would be right to ignore this condition.[6]

Admission into Christ's family, the Church, is something which happens once and for all time, and, therefore, baptism cannot be repeated. If, however, there is doubt as to whether a person has already been baptized, the Prayer Book makes provision for conditional baptism. Baptism can occur at any time during a person's life, and some Protestant bodies are insistent that it should not occur until the candidate has reached years of discretion and can make his baptismal vows for himself. The Church of England, however, while prepared to administer baptism to a candidate of any age, has come down fairly and squarely in favour of infant baptism whenever possible. Article XXVII says that 'the Baptism of young Children is in any wise to be retained in the Church, as most agreeable with the institution of Christ', while the Prayer Book urges baptism not later than the first or second Sunday after birth.[7] If a minister refuses or delays to baptize an infant, the parents or guardians may apply for directions to the bishop of the diocese in accordance with Canon B22. No delay or refusal is permitted in the case of an infant who is weak or in danger of death. It is, moreover, an offence for a minister to take or demand any fee for baptizing.[8]

In the case of infants the Prayer Book contemplates total immersion as the normal method, but states that if 'the Child is weak, it shall suffice to pour Water upon it',[9] and today it seems to be assumed that nearly every child is weak, for immersion is in practice the exception rather than the rule. In the case of adults it would seem that the Prayer Book expresses no preference[10] between immersion and affusion.

The appropriate occasion for baptism is on Sunday at public worship.[11] The Prayer Book indicates that it should take place

5. Rubric at the beginning of the Public Baptism of such as are of Riper Years.
6. See the observation on necessity, p. 70 *ante*.
7. Rubric at the beginning of The Private Baptism of Children.
8. Baptismal Fees Abolition Act, 1872 (35 & 36 Vict., c.36).
9. Rubric in the Public Baptism of Infants.
10. Rubric in The Ministration of Baptism to such as are of Riper Years.
11. Canon B21.

immediately after the second lesson at either Morning Prayer or Evening Prayer on a Sunday,[12] and, though for many years baptism tended to be a social event occurring on a week-day in the presence only of invited guests, of recent years the practice of baptizing at the appropriate time has been largely revived. If the baptism takes place in church, the administration is followed immediately by the signing of the Cross on the forehead of the person baptized, in token that thereafter 'he shall not be ashamed to confess the faith of Christ crucified, and manfully to fight under his banner against sin, the world and the devil, and to continue Christ's faithful soldier and servant unto his life's end'.[13] The signing with the Cross, however, forms no part of the actual baptism.[14] It marks the reception of the candidate into the congregation of Christ's flock, and, if the baptism is private, as it may properly be in a case of urgency, the candidate is not signed with the Cross on the occasion of the baptism, but on a later occasion in church.[15]

Candidates for baptism should have three sponsors—for a male candidate, two godfathers and one godmother, and for a female candidate, two godmothers and one godfather,[16] and, by Canon B23, they must be persons who have been baptized and confirmed, unless the minister dispenses with this requirement. When three sponsors cannot conveniently be had, one godfather and one godmother are sufficient. If the candidate is too young to answer for himself, the godparents make the affirmations for him, and it becomes their duty to see that the candidate is educated in the Christian faith and brought to the bishop for confirmation. The father and the mother may be godparents,[17] and, in a case of urgency, there need be no godparents. It is the godparents, if there be any, who name the candidate, and the name by which a person is baptized becomes his Christian name, though it may be altered at confirmation, or, it would seem, at will.[18]

---

12. Rubrics at the beginning of The Public Baptism of Infants and The Private Baptism of Children.
13. The Public Baptism of Infants.   14. Canon B25.
15. The Private Baptism of Infants.
16. The Public Baptism of Infants, and Canon B23.
17. Canon B23. There must be at least one other godparent.
18. See Halsbury, vol. 14. para. 1000, and vol. 35, para. 1174, together with Canon B27.

All baptisms are to be registered as soon as they have occurred.[19]

In the case of a person baptized in infancy, confirmation is deferred until such time that as he is thought to be able to affirm for himself what was affirmed on his behalf by his godparents at his baptism. In practice this age varies greatly, the two most common ages being about twelve or about sixteen. The Prayer Book and Canon B27 require that candidates for confirmation should be able to say the Creed, the Lord's Prayer, and the Ten Commandments, and also to answer questions based on the Catechism. In the case of persons who have not been baptized until they are of riper years it is not uncommon for their baptism to be followed immediately by their confirmation and then by their first Communion, all on the same occasion, the first two often taking place just before midnight on Easter Eve, and the third on Easter Day, just after midnight which ends the Eve has struck.

The precise theological significance of confirmation is also a matter of some dispute, and the Church of England, while insisting on its importance, is singularly silent as to its meaning. It is probably agreed that it is the bestowal of the Holy Spirit to strengthen the candidate in the performance of the baptismal vows which he has either just taken or else reaffirmed. It is as such commonly regarded as a completion of the rite of baptism, from which, in the West, it has got separated by reason of the growth in the custom of infant baptism. In the East, however, where infant baptism is also the norm, the infant is baptized and confirmed and receives the first Communion at a single service shortly after birth.

There is a difference of practice in Christendom concerning the person who may confirm. In some branches of the Church it is permissible for a priest to confirm, using for the purpose oil which has been blessed by the bishop. In the Church of England, however, confirmation is reserved to the bishop (or to another bishop acting on his behalf) and is performed by the laying on of hands accompanied by the prayer set forth in the Prayer Book, or other authorized forms of service.

The rubric at the end of the Order of Confirmation[20] states

---

[19]   Parochial Registers Act, 1812 (52 Geo. III, c.146).
[20]   The Order of Confirmation.

that no one is to be admitted to the Holy Communion until such time as he be confirmed, or be ready and desirous to be confirmed. Although the framers of this rubric did not contemplate the position today when Christians of other traditions are working closely with members of the Church of England, the rubric, strictly interpreted, is a bar to the admission of Nonconformists to Anglican altars. Canon B15A however enables baptized persons who are communicant members of other Churches which subscribe to the doctrine of the Holy Trinity to be admitted. The General Synod may by regulation authorize the admission of other baptized persons.

This is clearly not the place to discuss in any depth eucharistic doctrine;[21] but since the law has been concerned to uphold in the Church of England doctrine which is claimed to be at once Catholic and Reformed and mould the Church's liturgy to conform with these concepts, it is impossible altogether to avoid theological considerations, for they lie at the root of much of the law.

It is clear that Transubstantiation (at least, as understood by the Roman Church in the sixteenth and seventeenth centuries) is incompatible with Anglican doctrine and is expressly repudiated by Article XXVII of the Thirty-nine Articles. It is also clear that it was against the policy of the reformers to countenance non-communicating Masses, that is, celebrations at which only the priest receives the elements, and a rubric at the end of the Order for the Administration of the Lord's Supper in the Book of Common Prayer states that there shall be no celebration 'except there be a convenient number to communicate with the Priest, according to his discretion'.[22] It is clear that it is intended that all communicants, and not merely the celebrant, should communicate in both kinds, receiving both the bread and the wine after consecration. It is clear that the Church of England lays great emphasis on the sacramental character of what occurs, in that the outward and visible sign of

[21] The reader is referred to theological works on the subject, of which there are many. In particular he is referred to Doctrine in the Church of England, being the Report of the Archbishops' Commission in 1922 (SPCK); *Belief and Practice*, by Will Spens (Longmans, Green & Co.); and, for a very full discussion in two volumes, *The Mystery of Faith*, by Maurice de la Taille (published in Latin, French, and English, the English version being published by Sheed and Ward).

[22] See p. 82 *post*.

the consecrated bread and wine, properly used, effectively conveys an inward and spiritual grace, by the strengthening and refreshing of our souls by the Body and Blood of Christ, which is given, taken, and eaten after an heavenly and spiritual manner.[23]

Beyond this, however, Englishmen are left very much to their own tastes and devices as to their understanding of the nature of the sacrament. The sacrificial idea is discernible, as is also the commemorative.[24] There are traces (but no more)[25] of Virtualism and Receptionism[26] in some of the language employed. The repudiation of Transubstantiation does not involve the rejection of the Real Presence, and, indeed, in their more refined forms, we may eventually be in the joyful position of discovering that there is no difference between the two. Three of four centuries have shown that there is ample room within the Church of England for considerable developments in the field of eucharistic doctrine.[27] Meanwhile, it is probably true to say that all that is required of members of the Church is that they should accept that, by partaking faithfully of the sacrament, they are by grace permitted to appropriate to themselves the benefits won for them on Calvary, and they are not committed to any view as to how precisely this is effected. The famous answer of Queen Elizabeth I when questioned about the nature of the sacrament probably still reflects all that the average English churchman is prepared to say or that the law requires of him:

> 'Twas God the Word that spake it,
> He took the Bread and brake it;
> And what the word did make it;
> That I believe and take it.

[23] Catechism and Article XVII.

[24] See p. 66 *ante*.

[25] No more, when one considers the impossibility of expressing the sacramental without using language acceptable to Virtualists and Receptionists (see footnote 26).

[26] In both Virtualism and Receptionism it is held that the bread and wine remain unchanged. In Virtualism it is held that, by them, the virtue of the Body and Blood is received. In Receptionism it is held that by faith the true Body and Blood are received.

[27] Including an understanding that, in the sacrament, the faithful are associated not only with the sacrifice of Christ's death upon the Cross but also with the eternal offering of his life in Heaven.

That, in briefest outline, is the theological background against which the law must be set, if it is to be interpreted aright. It is interesting to note that, in a very minor particular, recognition is given to the diversity of views concerning the nature of the sacrament by Canon B8 permitting a choice of dress to the sacred ministers at a celebration of the Holy Communion, in which it is expressly stated in the preamble that the Church does not attach particular doctrinal significance to the diversities of vestures which may be worn. It is, however, to be noted that, while the Church may not attach any doctrinal significance to the vesture of the minister, it is more than probable that his choice of clothing will reflect the individual minister's theological inclinations.

One of the more frequent subjects of controversy concerns Reservation,[28] and opinion is divided as to its legality. It is difficult to see how it can be argued that Reservation of the consecrated elements is in itself in any way contrary to Anglican doctrine. The main doctrinal argument urged against Reservation is that Article XXV states that 'the Sacraments were not ordained of Christ to be gazed upon or to be carried about, but that we should duly use them', while Article XXVIII states that 'the Sacrament of the Lord's Supper was not by Christ's ordinance reserved, carried about, lifted up, or worshipped'. As has already been indicated,[29] the Thirty-nine Articles are to be interpreted in their literal and grammatical sense, and, so taken, no one would dispute the statement that there is no ordinance of Our Lord's concering the Reservation of the Sacrament, or, for that matter, concerning a large number of other practices, some of which are harmless and some laudable. Reservation is practised in other Churches of the Anglican Communion which share the doctrines of the Church of England. It was approved by all three Houses of the Church Assembly and would without doubt have been lawful under the deposited Prayer Book of 1928, if that Book had not been rejected by the House of Commons; and, as long ago as 1900 both archbishops expressed the view that it was theologically permissible. They also, after taking advice,

---

[28] i.e. setting aside some of the consecrated elements.
[29] See p. 60 *ante*.

doubted its legality; and it is perfectly true that not everything that is doctrinally permissible is necessarily lawful, though in this instance it is submitted that further consideration has shown that the archbishops' doubts are not substantiated.

Those who argue that, whatever be the doctrinal position, Reservation is against the law, base their case in the main on the rubric at the end of the Order for the Administration of the Holy Communion in the Book of Common Prayer which directs that 'if any of the Bread and Wine remain unconsecrated, the Curate shall have it for his own use (a provision which is clearly out of date now); but if any remain of that which was consecrated, it shall not be carried out of the Church, but the Priest, and such other of the Communicants as he shall then call unto him, shall, immediately after the Blessing, reverently eat and drink the same'. It is thought that the framers of this rubric did not have in mind the practice of Reservation, but were concerned to prevent the profanities of Puritan ministers who had so little regard for the act of consecration that they did not hesitate to take home for their ordinary personal consumption, not only the unexpended part of the unconsecrated elements, but even whatever remained of the consecrated elements. But, whatever the reason for the rubric, it has been argued with force that it provides a clear prohibition against anything other than the immediate consumption of the consecrated elements.

There would be more weight in this argument if the rubric were itself a statutory enactment. But, as has already been indicated,[30] though it has statutory authority, it is not in itself an Act of Parliament. It is a clerical directive and should be interpreted as such. The main purpose for which Reservation is required today is for the Communion of the sick and sometimes for others who cannot be present in church at the time of the consecration. A strong case can be made for the view that a clerical directive aimed at Puritanical profanities ceases to have force in circumstances not contemplated by its authors.

But, be that as it may, an even stronger argument in favour of Reservation can often be advanced in particular cases based on the doctrine of necessity.[31] It is often impossible in modern

[30]. See pp.59 and 60 *ante*.
[31]. See p. 70 *ante*.

conditions for the sick to receive the sacrament unless it has been reserved, for in populous districts a single-handed priest cannot spare the time for the individual sick-room celebrations contemplated in the Prayer Book in its service for the Communion of the Sick. In such cases (and there may well be others) necessity dictates that there should be Reservation in some seemly manner[32] in the church.[33] It is also to be noted, on both the doctrinal and the legal issue, that there was until 1967 still extant that part of the Brawling Act, 1553,[34] which provided for the protection of the sacrament and for the receptacle housing it; and this is an indication that the possibility of lawful Reservation is contemplated by Parliament.

As to the elements to be consecrated: Canon B17 lays upon the churchwardens the duty of providing 'a sufficient quantity of bread and of wine for the number of communicants that shall from time to time receive the same,' while a rubric at the end of the Order for the Administration of Holy Communion states that 'to take away all occasion of dissensions, and supersition, which any persons hath or might have concerning the Bread and Wine, it shall suffice that the Bread be such as is usual to be eaten; but the best and purest Wheat Bread that conveniently may be gotten'. Wine has its common meaning, namely, fermented, alcoholic grape-juice; unfermented grape-juice is not permissible.[35] Until recently it was argued[36] that the now frequent use of unleavened wafers instead of ordinary baker's

---

32. For the manner of Reservation, see p. 117 *post*.

33. For a full consideration of the law see *Bishopwearmouth (Rector and Churchwardens)v. Adey* (1958), 3 All E.R. 441. See also *Re Lapford* (1954), 2 All E.R. 310 (in the Consistory Court of Exeter) and on appeal (1954), 3 All E.R. 484. The reasoning of the judgment in the Court of the Arches presents great difficulties and is *discussed in the Bishopwearmouth case. See also Re St. Mary's, Tyne Dock (1954), 2 All E.R. 339 and Re St. Nicholas, Plumstead (1961), 1 All E.R. 298. In Re St. Peter and St. Paul, Leckhampton (1967), 3 All E.R. 1057* it was held that since the rubric in the Book of Common Prayer was not repeated in the alternative service of that date (see now The Alternative Service Book 1980) a celebration in accordance with one of the new services is not governed by the rubric in the Book of Common Prayer. In such cases it is submitted that reservation is lawful. It would therefore seem absurd to suggest that criticism can be levelled any longer at reservation, even after a service in accordance with the Book of Common Prayer. For the method of reserving see Chapter X *post*.

34. Act I Mar., sess. 2, c.3, repealed by the Criminal Law Act 1967 (15 & 16 Eliz.II. c 58).

35. Canon B17.

bread was unlawful, having regard to the rubric, though it is to be noted that all the rubric in terms says is that ordinary bread shall *suffice*. But the Prayer Book (Miscellaneous Provisions) Measure, 1965,[37] resolved the controversy by granting that unleavened bread may be used. It is almost certainly what our Lord used at the Last Supper. Oddly enough, no argument seems to have arisen concerning the propriety, legal or theological, of using individual wafers or individual cubes of bread.[38] Both are frequently used, yet neither lends itself conveniently to the breaking and sharing which one associates with the sacrament.

Since the celebration is the corporate act of the whole Church, it is required (as has been noted)[39] that the people should communicate as well as the priest. The rubric has generally been understood to require at least three communicants besides the priest. The actual wording of the rubric, however, is that there shall 'be a convenient number to communicate with the Priest, according to his discretion. And there be not above twenty persons in the Parish of discretion to receive the Communion: yet there shall be no Communion, except four (or three at the least) communicate with the Priest.' This is almost certainly an indication that three is the minimum in any parish, whatever its size, and that in the larger parishes the priest at his discretion may require more than three; but the looseness of the wording is an example of how impossible it is to interpret rubrics as though they were statutes, for a strict interpretation would lead one to the absurd conclusion that the requirement of three communicants is confined to the smaller parishes, while in the larger parishes the number depends entirely on the minister's discretion and could be less than three. In practice it is by no means uncommon for there to be but one other person, namely the server, besides the priest.

According to the rubrics, those who intend to communicate shall signify their intention to the curate at least some time the day before. It is very doubtful whether this rubric is ever obeyed today.

'In Cathedral and Collegiate Churches, and Colleges, where

---

36. See *Ridsdale* v. *Clifton*, [1877] 2 P.D. 276.
37. No. 3. Now repealed. Canon B17 continues to permit the use of unleavened bread.
38. There is a hint of it in *Elphinstone* v. *Purchas*, [1870] L.R. 3 A & E. 66.
39. See p.77 *ante*.

there are many Priests and Deacons, they shall all receive the
Communion with the Priest every Sunday at the least', and
'every Parishioner shall communicate at the least three times a
year, of which Easter to be one'[40]. If the modern Anglican
regards these minimal obligations as very light, his seventeenth-
century forebears may have regarded them as heavy. Before the
Reformation, attendance at Mass was frequent, but reception
of the Holy Communion was infrequent, and for most persons
not more often than once a year.

According to the Book of Common Prayer, the curate is to
repel 'an open and notorious evil liver' and any who has 'done
wrong to his neighbours by word or deed, so that the
Congregation be thereby offended', and the expulsion is to
continue effective until such time as the offender repents. 'The
same order shall the Curate use with those with those betwixt
whom he perceiveth malice and hatred to reign; not suffering
them to be partakers of the Lord's Table, until he know them to
be reconciled', and, if one be prepared to be reconciled and not
other, the one is to be admitted and the other repelled.[41] These
rubrics have now been replaced[42] by the following one:

if a Minister be persuaded that anyone of his Cure who presents
himself to be a partaker of the Holy Communion ought not to be
admitted thereunto by reason of malicious and open contention with
his neighbours, or other grave and open sin without repentance, he
shall give an account of the same to the Bishop of the Diocese, or other
the Ordinary of the place, and therein obey his order and direction,
but so as not to refuse the Sacrament to any until in accordance with
such order and direction he shall have called him and advertised him
that in any wise he presume not to come to the Lord's Table; Provided
that in case of grave and immediate scandal to the Congregation the
Minister shall not admit such person, but shall give an account of the
same to the Ordinary within seven days after at the furthest and
therein obey his order and directions provided also that before issuing
his order and direction in relation to any such person the Ordinary
shall afford to him an opportunity for interview.

[40.] Rubrics at the end of the Order for the Administration of the Holy Communion.
'Every parishioner' presumably means every *confirmed* parishioner. This is another
example of the loose drafting displayed by the rubrics. See also Canons B13 and
B15.

[41.] Rubrics at the beginning of the Order for the Administration of the Holy
Communion. See also Canon 26 of 1603.

[42.] Prayer Book (Miscellaneous Provisions) Measure, 1965 (No. 3); repealed. Now
see Canon B16, which adds the proviso in the final sentence of the quotation.

A minister purporting to act under the former rubrics had to be very circumspect, not only because charity dictates that anyone desirous of coming to the Lord's Table should, if possible, be permitted to do so, but also because this is enjoined by the Sacrament Act, 1547,[43] and a wrongful repulsion by the minister could involve him in serious litigation in the temporal courts, among other things for defamation. A person was not 'an open and notorious evil liver' simply because, like everyone else, he was a sinner. Even open breaches of the Church's code of conduct did not justify such a description and (for example) a divorced person living with his legal second spouse while his first partner was still living could not be regarded as coming within the condemnation of the rubric, nor could someone living with his deceased wife's sister.[44] It is apprehended that the same care is required under the new rubric, both by the minister and by the bishop, in the interpretation of the words 'grave and open sin' and 'grave and immediate scandal'. It is only something which causes great scandal and offence which can justify so strong a measure as repulsion from the altar.

The Prayer Book contemplates that there shall be a collection taken at the offertory,[45] and a rubric directs that the money so taken 'shall be disposed of to such pious and charitable use, as the Minister and Church-wardens shall think fit. Wherein if they disagree, it shall be disposed of as the Ordinary shall appoint.' It should be noted that, whereas other collections are under the control of the Parochial Church Council,[46] the collection taken at the offertory is at the disposal of the minister and churchwardens. Of course, a collection taken for a specific purpose which has been communicated to the donors forms a trust fund and may be devoted to no other purpose, though the offertory is not the occasion on which such a collection should be made, unless its purpose is pious and charitable. But, apart from that the minister and churchwardens have a complete discretion, provided that the purpose to which they put the collection is both pious *and* charitable.[47] In the prayer for the

---

[43.] 1 Edw. VI, c.1.

[44.] See *Banister* v. *Thompson* (1908), p.362; and *R. v. Dibdin (1910), p.57; and Thompson* v. *Dibdin* (1912), A.C. 533.

[45.] It should perhaps be made clear that the offertory is the offering by the people of the elements which are to be consecrated. The term does not refer to the monetary collection taken at that time.

[46.] See Chapter IV *ante*.

Church, the expression *alms* refers to the money collected at the offertory; but the expression *oblations* is thought to refer, not to the elements, but to church-dues now obsolete.[48] If this be correct, then, on the occasions when there is no collection, the whole reference to *alms and oblations* should be omitted from the prayer for the Church.

Without the permission of the bishop the Holy Communion may not be celebrated in private houses, except in the case of ministering to the sick, when the requirement of there being at least three communicants still holds, save in the event of there being a contagious disease.[49] It may be celebrated in private chapels with the permission of the bishop.[50]

Only a priest (that is, one who has been ordained priest by a bishop) can celebrate the Holy Communion.[51] It pertains, however, to the office of a deacon to assist the priest in divine service and to read the Scriptures in church and specially to assist at the distribution of the Holy Communion.[52] It is customary for the deacon to read the Gospel during the service of Holy Communion. It is also customary for him to administer the chalice, while the priest administers the paten. There is, however, no reason why the deacon should not administer the paten. In accordance with ancient custom, a subdeacon reads the Epistle at High Mass.[53] Lay involvement in the distribution is also allowed by virtue of Canon B12. The sacrament may be distributed by a person specially authorized to do so by the bishop acting under the regulations of the General Synod; and, subject to the bishop's direction, a lay person may read the Epistle and the Gospel at the invitation of the minister.

[47.] These are terms of art with a long history of litigation in Chancery. For guidance as to what may or may not be done under this rubric the reader is referred to the *Opinions of the Legal Board*.

[48.] See *A New History of the Book of Common Prayer*, by Procter and Frere.

[49.] Rubrics in the Communion of the Sick in the Book of Common Prayer. There is no similar provision in the Alternative Service Book, and the limitation in the Book of Common Prayer may perhaps be regarded as today of no effect. Certainly in practice a celebration by the priest with no one present other than the patient is quite common. It is to be noted also that the prohibition refers only to a celebration and has no reference to an administration from the Reserved Sacrament.

[50.] See p.55 *ante*.

[51.] Canon B12.

[52.] Ordinal.

[53.] The roles of deacon and subdeacon are frequently assumed at High Mass by priests.

IX

HOLY MATRIMONY

According to the Book of Common Prayer,[1] Holy Matrimony 'is an honourable estate, instituted of God in the time of man's innocency, signifying unto us the mystical union that is betwixt Christ and his Church'. This does not mean that the *object* of matrimony is to signify this union. It means rather that it is an example in the so-called 'natural' order of things of how that natural order reflects the heavenly, in the same way as man, being made in the image of God, should reflect something of the divine. Marriage is thus sacramental in character, though Article XXV[2] states that it (and others) 'are not to be counted for Sacraments of the Gospel . . . for that they have not any visible sign or ceremony ordained of God'.[3] But, whether one cares to call marriage a sacrament or something in the nature of a sacrament, depending on whether or not one's definition of a sacrament is something ordained by Christ and having its visible sign ordained by God, marriage is something more than a contract. In this both the temporal law of England and canon law agree. Marriage is not a contract; but it springs from a contract and is the union of one man with one woman for life. The contract is one which must have been freely entered upon by both parties to the marriage, and they must both have been free to make the contract, neither being already the spouse of another, nor suffering from any disability, such as lack of due age or unsoundness of mind; and they must have been free to make the contract *with each other*, not being within the prohibited degrees of affinity; and it must have been their common intention that the union should last until one of them should die, and should be a union to the exclusion of all others.

For centuries Church and State were at one over the nature

[1.] Solemnization of Matrimony.

[2.] Thirty-nine Articles.

[3.] Cf. the Catechism, where the two sacraments 'as equally necessary to salvation' are those ordained by Christ. See Chapter VIII, *ante*, p.72.

of marriage, for the State simply followed Western canon law in the matter. But with the introduction by the State of divorce (in the modern sense of the term) a divergence has arisen which, though it *can* be reconciled with the statement that the law of the Church and the law of the State are one, renders the reconciliation in this respect somewhat strained.

Put briefly, both agree that marriage springs from a contract; but, whereas the State must now be taken to say that what results from this contract is a new status, the Church continues to maintain that what results is something more than status - something akin to the relationship existing between parent and child or of brother and sister. Though the expression relationship is not a happy one, it is used here to denote something different from status. Mr. Sheed[4] puts it this way, that 'relationship differs from status in this: that it is a God-made thing, which man cannot alter. God alone can bring it into being.' But status depends 'upon the will of the State', and 'status can be varied *by the State'*.

Once it is recognized that it is a theological tenet[5] of the Church that the relationship arising on marriage is a God-given relationship, many of the misunderstandings concerning the Church's attitude to divorce are dissipated. On this view, it is simply not within the Church's competence to recognize a divorce as something which sets the parties free to contract new marriages with other partners. Wide as are the powers delegated to the Church by our Lord, the Church's authority is still only a delegated authority and cannot be exercised outside the framework of the divine law.[6] It is no more within the competence of the Church to declare that a man and a woman who have contracted a valid marriage are now no longer husband and wife than it is within her competence to declare that the relationship of parent and child is dissolved. It is, however, within the Church's competence to legislate with regard to incidentals, and to vary that legislation from time to time and place to place. The form, time, and place of the ceremony, for example, are all matters about which the church

---

4. Nullity of Marriage, by F. I. Sheed (Sheed and Ward), in which the Roman Catholic view is admirably and succinctly stated.
5. At least, of the Western Catholic Church.
6. See Chapter I *ante*.

may legislate. Nor does the church deny the right of the State to terminate the legal consequences of marriage. Just as the State has the right to remove a child from the control of a parent who has abused that control, so the State by a decree of divorce may grant freedom from the legal chains which bind together a husband and wife. But, says the Church, though the legal nexus between parent and child may be destroyed, they still remain parent and child; and, though the legal nexus of marriage be dissolved, the parties still remain husband and wife, and, therefore, each is incapable during the lifetime of the other of contracting a true marriage with another partner.[7]

With the introduction in the nineteenth century of divorce into the secular law of England the views of the Church and State, for centuries identical, have now diverged. The State regards those whose marriage has been dissolved as free to contract a fresh marriage. The Church does not. There are those who argue that it is not open to an Established Church to take a line at variance with that of the State with which it is identified, and that the secular legislation of the nineteenth century introducing divorce must be taken as simply a part of the overall legislation springing from the Reformation and effecting a change from the position before the Reformation. Such extreme erastianism, however, is quite unacceptable to those who take the Western Catholic view of the nature of marriage and who further regard the Church's authority as only a delegated authority from Christ and limited by the scheme of the divine framework. To them such a second union simply is not theologically a marriage, whatever its legal consequences, and the marriage service cannot be used to hallow it.

The tension here between Church and State, with its consequent threat to the Establishment, is obvious. It is, however, complicated by the fact that not all churchmen accept the theology of the Western Catholic position, but are prepared to recognize such second unions as theologically valid marriages. In practice, the tension has been eased by a frank recognition of the differences which exist with regard to the nature of marriage - a recognition which has led to a measure, not of compromise, but of mutual forbearance. Thus, although there is in general a legal obligation on a minister to marry those

---

7.   But see p. 3 *ante*.

who are entitled by law to be married in his church,[8] he is by statute[9] relieved of this obligation in the case where there has been a divorce and the former partner of one of the parties is still living. On the other hand, he may not refuse Holy Communion to a person solely on the ground that such a person has contracted a second union after the dissolution of his first union by divorce, for, since the secular law permits such a union and regards it as a marriage, those taking advantage of the permission cannot be regarded as open and notorious evil livers within the meaning of the rubric before the Communion service.[10] This tension between Church and State on the question of divorce does not exist, save in one respect, with regard to nullity. A decree of divorce (in the modern sense) is the dissolution of an undoubted marriage. A decree of nullity is simply a declaration that what appears to be a marriage is in fact no marriage. This may arise for a number of reasons; but a distinction must be drawn between marriages void *ab initio* and those which are merely voidable. An apparent marriage may be void on any one of six grounds, namely: where at the time of the ceremony one of the parties was already married; where the parties were not respectively male and female; where the parties were within the prohibited degrees of affinity or consanguinity; where the ceremony of marriage was defective in form; where one of the parties was too young; and where the ceremony was, and was intended to be, merely a mock ceremony. A marriage, however, is voidable and not void on the following grounds; that one of the parties is impotent; that one of the parties did not validly consent to the marriage whether in consequence of duress, mistake, unsoundness of mind or otherwise; that one of the parties was suffering from a mental disorder so as to be unfitted for marriage; that at the time of the ceremony one of the parties was suffering from a communicable venereal disease; that at the time of the ceremony the woman was pregnant by another man; that, since the ceremony, there has been a wilful refusal by one of the parties ever to consummate the marriage.

Whereas a void marriage is one which does not exist at all, a

8. *Argar v. Holdsworth* [1758] 2 Lee 515; *Davis* v. *Black*, [1841] 1 Q.B. 900; *R.* v. *James*, [1850] 3 Car. and Kir. 167, C.C.R.
9. Matrimonial Causes Act, 1965, (13 & 14 Eliz. II. c.72), s.8(2).
10. Book of Common Prayer. *Thompson v. Dibdin* (1912), A.C. 533 H.L.

voidable marriage is one which must be taken to exist unless and until it is declared void by a court of competent jurisdiction, and no one may impugn such a marriage except a party to it. Thus, if, for example, one of the parties is impotent, no one other than the parties may impugn the validity of the marriage, and usually only the deprived party will do so.[11]

Church and State agree as to nullity and as to the distinction between a void and a voidable marriage, save in respect of a marriage which the State is prepared to treat as voidable on the ground of a wilful refusal to consummate. While the Church recognizes impotence as a ground for declaring a marriage voidable, and while in many cases a wilful refusal to consummate helps to provide evidence of impotence, the Church finds difficulty in regarding wilful refusal as in itself a ground for nullity. This is because the canon law has always considered that is essential for nullity that the ground on which such a declaration is based should already have been in existence *at the time* of the ceremony. Nothing arising thereafter can affect the validity of the ceremony in which the parties take each other for better or for worse until death do them part.[12] A wilful refusal to consummate is something which arises *after* the ceremony of marriage, and it is the only ground for nullity recognized by the secular law[13] which does arise after the ceremony. The logic of the Church's position is clear, if one grants the premiss that theologically a marriage is completed by the parties accepting each other as man and wife. It has, however, at times been argued that theologically a marriage is not a *fait accompli* until consummation. If this view were ultimately to prevail, the attitude of Church and State with regard to nullity would be reconciled.[14]

---

[11] At one time it was thought that the party who was impotent could not institute a suit for nullity and that such a suit could be instituted only by the other (or deprived) party. It seems, however, that this was not the law in England, whatever it may have been elsewhere. See *Harthan* v. *Harthan* (1948). 2 All E.R. 639, where the subject is exhaustively reviewed in the Court of Appeal.

[12] Book of Common Prayer, marriage service.

[13] Matrimonial Causes Act, 1973 (21 & 22 Eliz. II, c. 18), s. 12(b).

[14] See *Lacey, Marriage in Church and State* (revised ed. 1947), pp. 198 et seq.; see also *The Church and The law of Nullity of Marriage*, being the Report of a Commission appointed by the Archbishops of Canterbury and York in 1949 at the request of the Convocations.

This is not the place for a detailed exposition of either the theology or the law relating to marriage. For these, recourse must be had to theological works or legal textbooks. In the exercise of her delegated authority to legislate concerning incidentals, the Church of England will not recognize as a valid marriage anything which does not comply with current secular legal requirements. Equally, save in respect of divorced persons (and probably of persons whose marriages have been annulled on the ground of wilful refusal to consummate), she does recognize the validity of marriages celebrated in some fashion recognized by law other than according to the rites and ceremonies of the Church of England. Since a marriage arises by the mutual agreement of the parties, who, being free to do so, take each other for life to the exclusion of all others, it is open to the church to content herself with any formula which satisfies this basic requirement, and so, in England, the Church recognizes as fully as does the State the validity of marriages in Register Offices or in accordance with the requirements of other religious bodies,[15] and, in respect of marriages according to the rites and ceremonies of the Church of England, she requires compliance with the requirements of the secular law.[16] It will suffice here to notice only a few points.

It seems probable that every parishioner is entitled to marriage in church after banns, whether the parties are members of the Church of England or not, save possibly where neither party has been baptized. It is, however, worth noting that residence is a condition precedent to the publication of banns, and that residence does not occur simply by leaving a suitcase in the parish. Marriage after licence, however, is a privilege and not a right, and may be refused by the licensing authority. There are two sorts of licence, both of which obviate

[15] That is why, in England, when the parties have already been married in a Register Office and then desire a service in church, some adaptation of the service in the Book of Common Prayer is required in order to make it clear that a valid marriage had already occurred before the parties arrived at the church. The situation is different from that which arises sometimes abroad, where the Roman Catholic Church, in the exercise of the divine authority delegated to the Church in that country, refuses to recognize for her flock the secular ceremony upon which the State insists and so regards the subsequent ceremony in church as the effective marriage.

[16] For these see Halsbury, vol. 14, paras. 1006-1040.

the necessity for banns. There is the common licence, issued by or on the authority of the chancellor of the diocese, which simply dispenses with the necessity for banns. There is also the special licence of the Archbishop of Canterbury (being a remnant of the old legatine jurisdiction and thus operative in both provinces, having been perpetuated by the Ecclesiastical Licences Act, 1533[17]), which authorizes a marriage at any time and in any place, including places not otherwise licensed for marriages. A certificate from a superintendent registrar also dispenses with the necessity for banns.[18]

The marriage service should be conducted by a priest, for it involves the giving of a blessing; but it is generally thought to be lawful if conducted by a deacon.[19] It is envisaged that it should be followed by the Holy Communion, and the rubric at the end of the marriage service emphasizes this. The service should be in accordance with the Book of Common Prayer or other authorized form of service and the certificate which the minister afterwards gives certifies that it was solemnized according to the rites and ceremonies of the Church of England. The alternative version provided by the deposited Prayer Book of 1928 has no legal authority, though it is, in fact, frequently used, and it is to be hoped that it is sufficiently near to an authorised version for a court to decide, if the point should ever be raised, that the marriage was lawfully solemnized.

The law of England lays down strict requirements, both of substance and of form, for the celebration of a valid marriage. These are to be found in legal textbooks, and reference has been made here only to those aspects of marriage which closely concern the canon law. Failure to comply with these legal requirements can easily invalidate an apparent marriage in the eyes of the temporal law; and, since the Church requires compliance with the temporal law before she will recognize a marriage as canonically valid, the consequences of laxity in the

---

17. 25 Hen. VIII, c.21.
18. Marriage Act, 1949 (12 & 13 Geo. VI, c.76), s.78 (1).
19. R. v. *Millis*, [1844] 10 Cl. and Fin. 534; *Cope* v. *Barber*, [1872] L.R. 7 C.P. 393, *obiter* at p.403. Perhaps very much attention should not be paid to the former case. Willes J. does not seem to have realized that every priest is a deacon. The authorities are far from clear; but, if a clear case were to arise, it seems almost certain that a marriage at which a deacon officiated would be held to be valid.

observance of these requirements, if sufficient to invalidate the ceremony, can be very serious, both spiritually and temporally. Ministers of the Church, both in that capacity and also in their capacity as marriage-officers of the State, have a heavy responsibility towards those who come to them to be married, and they may unwittingly do a grave disservice to them unless they are careful with regard to the legal requirements, particularly with regard to residence and the form of service.

X

THE OTHER OFFICES AND PENANCE

The word *office* comes from the Latin *officium*, meaning a *duty*, the divine office being the worship enjoined as a duty. In the Middle Ages the duty was an onerous one so far as religious (monks, friars, and nuns) were concerned; and consisted daily of Matins, said in the middle of the night, and Lauds, Prime, Terce, Sext, None, Vespers, and Compline, said at fixed hours throughout the day. At the Reformation these disappeared from the official formularies of the Church of England, their place being taken by the two daily offices of Morning Prayer and Evening Prayer, often called Matins and Evensong respectively. In the Anglican religious orders the old offices have been revived, usually in English, while Compline (in English) has again achieved a wide popularity, even outside conventual walls. There is nothing unlawful about such services, regarded as voluntary extras; but they have no official place in the worship of the Church of England as do the two daily offices of Matins and Evensong.

Although the word *office* is often used in contradistinction to the sacraments, the daily offices being treated as preparation for Holy Communion, the expression *daily offices* is also taken to include Matins, Holy Communion, and Evensong, as the constant offices of the Church, so as to distinguish them from the occasional offices, for use as the need arises. These are the services for Baptism, Confirmation, Holy Matrimony, Visitation of the Sick, Communion of the Sick, Churching of Women, and the Burial of the Dead. To these may be added the Litany and the Commination Service. All of these find their place in the Book of Common Prayer, as do also the Forms of Prayer to be used at Sea, the Ordinal (for the Making, Ordaining, and Consecrating of Bishops, Priests, and Deacons), and the Forms of Prayer for the Anniversary of the Day of Accession of the Reigning Sovereign. For special occasions, such as a Coronation or a day of national thanksgiving, or the enthronement of a bishop, special forms of service may be approved or used pursuant to Canons B4 and B5.

Consideration has already been given to Baptism, Confirmation, Holy Communion, and Holy Matrimony; and this chapter, so far as is necessary, will deal with Matins, Evensong, Visitation and Communion of the Sick, the Churching of Women, and the Burial of the Dead. Consideration will also be given to Penance though this can scarcely be described as an office. It is often known as the Sacrament of Penance. But, however one describes it, it calls for special consideration which can be accorded it in this chapter as conveniently as anywhere.

1. MORNING AND EVENING PRAYER

The Bishop may in certain circumstances authorize the minister of a parish church to dispense with the reading of Morning and Evening Prayer on any Sunday, on any principal Feast Day, or on Ash Wednesday or Good Friday. Otherwise 'the minister of the parish, together with all other ministers licensed to serve in the said parish, being at home and not otherwise reasonably hindered, shall resort to the church morning and evening, and, warning being given to the people by the tolling of the bell, say or sing the Common Prayers and on the appointed days the Litany.[1] For two centuries no deviations from the forms prescribed in the Prayer Book were permitted,[2] though the addition of hymns was held to be lawful and the service could lawfully be sung.[3] But now variations are permitted.[4] There is, however, no lawful authority for the use of the Revised Prayer

---

[1] Canon B11. Canon C26 directs bishops, priests and deacons to say daily the Morning and Evening Prayer, 'not being let by sickness or some other urgent cause'. See also the passage entitled 'Concerning the Services of the Church' in the Book of Common Prayer.

[2] Act of Uniformity 1662 (14 Car. II, c.4), and also the Act of Uniformity, 1558 (I Eliz., c.2), and Canon 14, of 1603.

[3] See *Hutchins* v. *Denziloe and Loveland*, [1792], 1 Hag. Con. 170 and *Read* v. *Bishop of Lincoln* (1892), A.C. 644, P.C.

[4] See Universities Tests Act, 1871 (34 & 35 Vict., c.37); Prayer Book (Tables of Lessons) Act, 1871 (34 & 35 Vict., c.37); Act of Uniformity Amendment Act, 1872 (35 & 36 Vict., c. 35); Revised Tables of Lessons Measure 1922 (12 & 13 Geo. V. No. 3); and Canon B5. Alternative forms of service are of course permitted by the Church of England (Worship and Doctrine Measure, 1974 (No.3)).

Book, 1928, or for the use, for example, of the Lectionary which the Convocations purported to authorize in 1961, for a resolution of Convocation cannot override an Act of Parliament. There is no place for a sermon at either Morning or Evening Prayer, both of which end with the Grace, it being anticipated that Morning Prayer would be followed by the Litany and then by the service for Holy Communion, where a place for the sermon is provided. When, as is common, Morning Prayer or Evening Prayer is followed after the Grace by a hymn, a sermon, another hymn (during which a collection is taken), and the Blessing, all that follows the Grace forms a separate service and since 1872 has been lawful,[5] as also is a sermon alone; preached on a separate occasion, if preceded by the Bidding Prayer.[6]

2. VISITATION AND COMMUNION OF THE SICK

Special provision is made in the Prayer Book in two separate services, the one for the Visitation of the Sick and the other for the Communion of the Sick. Both have tended to fall into desuetude.

In the case of the service for the Visitation of the Sick this is partly because it is in a form which appears to have lost its former appeal and partly because the soundness of its theology is questioned, particularly in its express statement that sickness is the visitation of God and in its implication that sickness is directly willed by him.

In the case of the service for the Communion of the Sick, the modern tendency has been more and more to substitute for it Communion from the Reserved sacrament. This has been partly on the purely practical ground that time does not permit of a separate celebration in each home where there is a sick person, and partly on the ground that theologically it is thought sounder to communicate the sick person from the elements consecrated at the common board of the community. We have already considered the legal aspects of this.[7] Canon B37

5. Act of Uniformity Amendment Act, 1872 (35 & 36 Vict., c.35), and Canon B1.
6. Canon B19.
7. Chapter VIII.

provides express permission for the celebration of the Holy Communion in a private house. The rubrics again emphasize the requirement that there should be at least three communicants besides the priest; but they dispense with this requirement if, by reason of the infectious nature of the illness, it is impossible of fulfilment; infection, however, is the only ground specified to justify the dispensation.

No other services for the sick are provided by the Prayer Book, but alternative forms of service for Unction or the Laying on of Hands may be used in accordance with Canon B37.

3. THE CHURCHING OF WOMEN

The full title of this service is *The Thanksgiving of Women after Childbirth, commonly called The Churching of Women.* Its popularity or otherwise seems to depend on locality and social conventions; but the language of the Prayer Book, both in the rubric at the beginning of the service and in the opening words to be uttered by the priest, is in form mandatory. It is, too, a priest and not a deacon who is indicated as the minister. It is not expressly stated, but seems to be implied, and is certainly commonly taken to be intended, that this should be the first public service to be attended by a woman after childbirth. The rubric at the end of the service directs that it is convenient that she should receive the Holy Communion, if there be a celebration. The same rubric also directs that she 'must offer accustomed offerings'.

4. BURIAL OF THE DEAD

Every parishioner, and everyone dying in the parish, is entitled by law to burial in the parish churchyard or burial ground, whether or not he was a member of the Church of England, or, indeed even a Christian. If one cannot speak of a dead person as having legal rights the matter may be restated by saying that the personal representatives and relatives of the deceased are entitled to claim burial for the body in such churchyard or burial ground[8] There is no right, except under faculty, to burial in the church itself or in any particular spot in

[8] See p.40 *ante*

the burial ground, or, except under faculty, to erect a tombstone.[9] The right to burial exists only provided there is still space in the ground for the burial. Canon B38 declares cremation to be lawful and permits cremated remains to be interred or deposited in consecrated ground. The right does not extend to the bodies of convicts executed in pursuance of the order of a court, and in such cases burial has to be within the precincts of the prison unless there is no convenient place therein and the Secretary of State has appointed some other place.[10]

In general, the minister of the parish where burial may be claimed is bound to conduct the funeral and to conduct it in accordance with the service in the Prayer Book or other authorised service, whether or not the deceased was a member of the Church of England. There are, however, three exceptions to this rule. The burial service is not to be said over the bodies of those who die unbaptized, or who have laid violent hands upon themselves, or who die ex-communicate.[11]

The expression *who have laid violent hands upon themselves*, has in practice been interpreted charitably to refer only to those who have deliberately committed suicide in circumstances which amounted to *felony-de-se* before the passing of the Suicide Act, 1961.[12] This Act, whereby it is no longer a crime to commit suicide, is silent on the subject of the burial of the bodies of those who have committed suicide, and it is, therefore, suggested that the rubric and Canon B38 are applicable in these circumstances. But it is rare in such cases for a coroner's inquest to record anything other than the kindly verdict that the deceased took his own life while the balance of his mind was temporarily disturbed, and this has in practice been treated as sufficient to take the case out of the ambit of the rubric and the Canon.

With regard to the unbaptized: it must be remembered that a baptism is lawful and sufficient, by whomsoever it may have been performed, provided it was with water and in the name of the Father and of the Son and of the Holy Ghost. Baptism

---

9.   See p.134 *post.*
10. Capital Punishment Amendment Act, 1868 (31 & 32 Vict., c.24).
11. Rubric at the beginning of the Burial Service; and Canon B38.
12. 9 & 10 Eliz. II, c.60.

within the Church of England is not a prerequisite. With regard to those who die excommunicate: this does not appear to have been a pressing issue for very many years; and now that excommunication is no longer included in the list of possible punishments in the Ecclesiastical Jurisdiction Measure, 1963.[13] it is doubtful whether this provision in the rubric, despite its repetition in Canon B38, has any further force.[14]

In all these three cases, however, the minister is permitted to use some other form of service approved by the ordinary, and he may also do so in other cases at the request of the relatives.[15] He is, too, in all cases bound on request to allow the burial of the body of a parishioner or of someone dying in the parish to be conducted in a seemly and Christian fashion, though not according to the Prayer Book, by anyone whom the relatives wish to conduct it, and he is also, at the wish of the relatives, bound to allow the burial to take place without any service.[16]

No minister is bound to conduct a burial in unconsecrated ground; but he is free to do so, if he wishes.[16]

5. PENANCE

The Sacrament of Penance, as it is called, is not one of the dominical[17] sacraments. It consists in confession with repentance and absolution and, when taking place privately, the performance of at least a token penance. This is not the place for a detailed study of so large a subject. It is, however, to be noted that the Book of Common Prayer makes provision (however emasculated) for both public and private penance.

In the service of Holy Communion there is a general confession followed by absolution. In the services for Morning and Evening Prayer there is also a general confession, followed by what the rubric terms 'The Absolution or Remission of sins to be pronounced by the Priest alone, standing: the people still

13. No. 1, s.49.
14. It may be that excommunication is still possible outside the Measure; and it may be, too, that a person excommunicated by a Church of competent jurisdiction outside England and dying in that state in England would still be caught by the rubric. See s.82 (4).
15. Burial Law Amendment Act, 1880 (43 & 44 Vict., c.41); Canon B38.
16. Ibid.
17. i.e. recorded in the Gospels as instituted by Our Lord.

kneeling.' Were it not for this intention, clearly declared in the rubric, someone coming fresh to the Prayer Book could excusably fail to realize that the actual words which the priest is to say are intended to be an absolution.

Private confession and absolution are enjoined by the Prayer Book in two places. In the Exhortation, seldom read, but directed to be read after the prayer for the Church in the service of Holy Communion, the minister exhorts the members of the congregation to examine their lives and conversations by the rule of God's commandments and then continues, '. . . if there be any of you, who by this means cannot quiet his own conscience herein, but requireth further comfort or counsel, let him come to me, or to some other discreet and learned Minister of God's Word, and open his grief; that by the ministry of God's Holy Word he may receive the benefit of absolution, together with ghostly counsel and advice . . .'. The other place where private confession and absolution are enjoined is in the Order for the Visitation of the Sick, where the sick person is to 'be moved to make a special confession of his sins, if he feels his conscience troubled with any weighty matter. After which confession the Priest shall absolve him (if he humbly and heartily desire it . . .)' The form of absolution there provided ends with the words, '. . . by [Christ's] authority committed to me, I absolve thee from all thy sins, In the Name of the Father and of the Son, and of the Holy Ghost. Amen.' It is thus apparent that a public and general confession is enjoined by the Prayer Book, and a private and particular one is indicated for any whose consciences remain troubled.[18]

The observance of secrecy concerning whatever is privately confessed, is, and always has been, one of the strictest obligations of a priest. It is further enjoined on him by Canon 113[19], though that canon purports to provide an exception in respect of 'such crimes as by the law of this realm [the priest's] own life may be called in question for concealing the same'. To what this exception refers is completely obscure, and in practice it is difficult to imagine any priest's divulging anything that he has learnt in the confessional, regardless of his own personal

[18] See also Canon B29.
[19] Of 1603. This has not been repealed.

safety, even assuming that that could be endangered. It is, furthermore, here submitted that the law of England confers an absolute privilege on a priest, whereby he is protected from being made to divulge in evidence what he has learnt in the confessional. Indeed, it is submitted that it is more than a privilege, and is, in fact, a prohibition. This view is based on the fact that the pre-Reformation canon law, unaltered in this respect by or since the Reformation, imposed an obligation of secrecy, and the Book of Common Prayer, with the statutory authority of the Act of Uniformity, 1662,[20] in enjoining private confession must be taken to have envisaged and embodied what was already the law on the subject. It is, however, only right to say that a contrary view has been advanced, though unsupported by binding authority, and has been expressed in textbooks on evidence and in judicial *obiter dicta*.[21]

---

20. 14 Car. II, c.4.
21. For a fuller discussion of this matter see an article by the author in the *Church Times* for 6 September 1963; a pamphlet entitled *The Seal of the Confessional and the Law of Evidence*, by Peter Winckworth (SPCK, 1952); and an article by Chancellor James R. Lindsay in *The Northern Ireland Legal Quarterly* for May 1959, entitled 'Privileged Communications: Communications with Spiritual Advisers'. For the contrary view see Cross on *Evidence* (2nd ed.), pp. 246 and 247.

XI

CHURCH PROPERTY

The property of the Church in England, like all other property in England, is either real or personal, and, as such, is basically governed by the same rules as other property.[1] But superimposed on the basic general law are many special incidents peculiar to ecclesiastical property, and it is with some of the more important of these that this chapter is concerned.

By far the most fundamental of these is the distinction between consecrated land and unconsecrated land.

Consecration must not be confused with dedication. Theologically it would seem that there is no difference between the two. Each is an act by man whereby he gives back to God what God has given or lent to man to do therewith what he will. By freely giving it back to God man in effect declares himself a trustee of the land for godly purposes.[2] But such a declaration, if expressed by dedication, amounts in law to no more than an expression of pious intention. To be clothed with legal effect it is necessary that there should be a sentence of consecration by the bishop, which occurs only after the freehold of the land has been secured. Though in practice there is invariably a religious ceremony devised and performed by the bishop, the legal effect of consecration is brought about by his signing the sentence of consecration which is then lodged in the Diocesan Registry. The effect of this is twofold: first, it brings the land and everything on it within the jurisdiction of the ordinary; and, secondly, it as it were freezes the land for ever by setting it aside *in sacros usus*. Thereafter only an Act of Parliament or a Measure

---

[1.] Broadly speaking, *real property* is land and *personal property* is any other sort of property. For the incidents attaching to these two sorts of property and the differences between them, which are considerable, recourse must be had to the appropriate legal textbooks. The subject is far too wide and complex for treatment here.

[2.] See the *Report of the Committee on Deconsecration* (of which the author was chairman), published by the Church Assembly in June 1961, headed 'C.A. Misc. 3'.

of the Church Assembly or General Synod can free the land for secular purposes.[3]

Consecration occurs most often in the case of a parish church or of a burial ground, and in such cases the jurisdiction of the ordinary is thereafter exercised by the chancellor in the Consistory Court by means of the faculty jurisdiction,[4] and any dealings with the land or with anything in it or on it require the authorization of the Court, which is sought by a petition for a faculty. Even so, a faculty cannot properly issue for any purpose inconsistent with the sacred uses to which the land has been consecrated. Chancellors are as liberal in their interpretion of what is consistent with sacred uses as circumstances permit; thus, leave has often been given for the erection of a church hall within the churchyard and for the granting of a right-of-way or for a way-leave across a churchyard. But there are limits beyond which liberality of interpretation cannot go, and, for example, permission has been refused for leave to use the site of a demolished church as a car-park.[5] Furthermore, disused burial grounds which have been closed by Order in Council have additional restrictions imposed upon them by statute,[6] as a result of which no building, other than an extension to the church, may be erected upon them.[7] On the other hand, there has been a number of statutory enactments, both public and private Acts of Parliament and Measures of the Church Assembly, which have in some instances modified or removed the restrictive effects in law of consecration. Thus, the Open Spaces Act, 1906,[8] permits the user, under the faculty, of a burial ground as an open space for the enjoyment of the public, and under the Pastoral Measure, 1983[9] it is possible in certain circumstances to use a redundant church or its site for secular purposes, while

[3.] It is said that it is not possible to convey the freehold of consecrated land. It is doubtful whether this is correct. But it is certainly of very little advantage to do so, for the land still remains consecrated and is still, therefore, under the jurisdiction of the ordinary and subject to all the limitations of consecration.

[4.] See Chapter XIV, p.134 *post*.

[5.] See *Re St. John's, Chelsea* (1962) 2 All E.R. 850 and the cases there cited. There is now provision in the Pastoral Measure 1983 (No. 1) for removing the legal effects of consecration.

[6.] Disused Burial Grounds Act, 1884 (47 & 48 Vict., c.72).

[7.] See *Re St. Mary's, Luton* (1966) 3 All E.R. 638 and *Re St. Anne's Church, Kew* (1976) 1 All E.R. 461. But the restrictions can now be overcome by a scheme under the Pastoral Measure 1983; see Section 30.

[8.] 6 Edw. VII, c.25.

[9.] No. 1.

planning legislation[10] gives powers to the appropriate Minister of the Crown to make orders greatly modifying the effects of consecration.

Though, when land is consecrated, it is usually for the purposes of a parish church or for a burial ground, there are plenty of instances where it has been consecrated for some other purpose, for example, for the purposes of a private chapel, or for the chapel of a college in Oxford or Cambridge, or for a cathedral. The act of consecration always brings the land or building within the jurisdiction of the ordinary; but the ordinary is not necessarily the bishop. In the case of the private chapel, as in the case of the parish church, the ordinary is the bishop, and thus the private chapel is brought within the faculty jurisdiction of the Consistory Court.[11] In the case of a cathedral, the ordinary may well be the dean and chapter,[12] and in the case of a college chapel, the Governing Body of the college may claim to be the ordinary.[13] But, whoever the ordinary may be, and whatever tribunal may be the appropriate one for enforcing the law, such places are not, as is sometimes imagined, above the law, though, outside a parish, those interested in its enforcement may be few in number, and the procedure for its enforcement may provide difficulties.

It is the act of consecration which, in the case of land or buildings, brings into operation in respect of them provisions of ecclesiastical law wich would otherwise have no application to them. To this rule there are, however, two exceptions. The unconsecrated curtilage[14] of a consecrated church has long been held to be subject to the faculty jurisdiction, and, although this was sometimes doubted, the Faculty Jurisdiction Measure, 1964,[15] has put the matter beyond dispute by a section declaring that this is so. The same Measure has also empowered the bishop to place any licensed but unconsecrated church

---

[10] See particularly the Town & Country Planning Act, 1971 (19 & 20 Eliz. II, c.78)
[11] This is not often realized, and the owners of private chapels sometimes find themselves seriously embarrassed by the limitation which this places on their freedom to deal with the chapel as they wish. If the full implications of consecration had been realized, resort might have been had to dedication rather than to consecration.
[12] See p.48 *ante.*   [13] See p.54 *ante.*
[14] Curtilage is the land around or immediately contiguous to, and belonging to, a building.
[15] No. 5, s.7.

within the faculty jurisdiction for such period as he thinks fit.[16]

Since consecrated lands and buildings are set aside in *sacros usus* for ever (or until legislation effects a release), they may thus be regarded as given back to God; but it is, nevertheless, human beings who have to deal with them and upon whom obligations and rights in respect of them devolve. It is the policy of English law always to seek some individual in whom the legal estate of property is vested. The beneficial interest of such an individual may well be limited, and it is a mistake to regard the legal owner as necessarily the person with the greatest beneficial interest. Thus, in the case of parish churches and their churchyards, the freehold is vested in the incumbent, but his rights are limited by a number of factors. He is, in fact, only a trustee.

His power of dealing with the land and building is restricted by the overriding control of his faculty jurisdiction, as a result of which his petition to do something with the church or churchyard (for example, to alter the line of a path across it) may be rejected, while the petition of some other person (for example, to erect a tombstone) may be granted, even though opposed by the incumbent. His powers are also restricted by the rights of others, such as the right of a parishioner to be buried in the churchyard,[17] and the rights of parishioners to cross the churchyard for the purpose of gaining access to the church at the time of divine worship. He may not, without permission, to fell trees has to be sought from the Parsonages Board of the diocese[18] and not from the Consistory Court. There is one beneficial right often not appreciated which the incumbent enjoys in the churchyard, and that is the right of herbage, whereby he may graze his sheep or cattle[19] in the churchyard.

---

16. Faculty Jurisdiction Measure, 1964, No.5, s.6. The main purpose of this provision is to meet the case, rare in the past but frequent today, where for many years a temporary and unconsecrated building (often a dual-purpose building, used as both a church hall and a church) will have to serve as a church for many years.

17. See p.40 *ante*.

18. Repair of Benefice Buildings Measure, 1972 (No. 2) The proceeds of sale of timber are to be applied primarily for the planting of new trees or for the maintenance of the fabric of the church.

19. And, it is apprehended, goats, geese, and horses, the word cattle not being confined to cows, sacred or otherwise. If only incumbents would exercise this right, they would often find a solution to the problem of the maintenace of the churchyard as well as deriving some small profit from the operation. One sensible incumbent grazes his donkey in the churchyard, tethering it by a long rope to a different tombstone each day. Elephants and giraffes, it is apprehended, could not be permitted, since they are not 'cattle'.

Although the incumbent is the legal owner of the churchyard and of the church, he does not become the legal owner of the tombstones or monuments therein, for, despite the maxim *quidquid plantatur solo, solo cedit,* a memorial (with its accoutrements) remains the property of the person who erects it, and after his death it either devolves upon the persons entitled under his will or on his intestacy or, possibly, passes to the heirs of the person commemorated.[20] But the rights of such owners are also severely limited by the faculty jurisdiction, for not only may the legal owners be refused permission to do something to the monument which they wish to do (for example, to add a further inscription), but others may be granted a faculty in respect of the monument against the wishes of the legal owners (for example, a faculty to remove the kerb round a grave).

While the rights of the incumbent as legal owner of the church and churchyard are so severely limited that in popular parlance he would scarcely be described as owner, so also are his liabilities limited. Save in some very rare instances, the obligation to maintain them in proper condition fell for many years upon the churchwardens, who discharged it out of church rates. Compulsory church rates, were, however, abolished by the Compulsory Church Rate Abolition Act, 1868,[21] and today the obligation rests upon the Parochial Church Council, but only to the extent of any funds which may be at its disposal.[22] The Parochial Church Council is to a like extent responsible also for the upkeep of the ornaments and furnishings of the church,[23] although the legal ownership of these is vested in the churchwardens.[24]

Much of the property of the Church consists of houses and land for its ministers. The law in this respect is far too

---

[20]. *Re St. Andrews, Thornhaugh,* (1976) 1 All E.R. 154.

[21]. 31 & 32 Vict., c.109.

[22]. Parochial Church Councils (Powers) Measure, 1956 (No.3).

[23]. Ibid.

[24]. Canon El. It should, however, be noted that a lay rector is usually liable for the upkeep of the chancel in which he usually has a right to sit. It is a liability which, together with the rectorship, runs with the land and it can be enforced by proceedings in the County Court: see Chancel Repairs Act, 1932 (22 & 23 Geo. V, c.20); see also Halsbury, vol. 14 para. 1106. The liability of the lay rector to maintan the chancel is now likely to be modified by legislation and the Law Reform Commission has already recommended a revision.

complicated and varied to receive detailed treatment here, and the reader who does not wish to pursue the study further[25] must be content with only a broad outline of the subject.

The archbishops, bishops, cathedral dignitaries, and the incumbents of parishes usually have official residences, of which the legal estate was usually vested in them for the purpose of their beneficial occupation, though today the residences of archbishops, bishops, and cathedral dignitaries are vested in the Church Commissioners;[26] but their rights, as one would expect, are limited in such a way as to ensure that the property is passed on undiminished to their successors. Thus, for example, an incumbent cannot dispose of his parsonage-house without the consent of the Parsonages Board of the diocese, the bishop, and the Church Commissioners,[27] while the proceeds of the sale of such property are retained as capital for the benefice, being perhaps expended on or towards the purchase of another residence for the incumbent, which in turn will pass to his successor.[28] The incumbent was formerly primarily responsible for the general upkeep of the property occupied by him, but it is now for the diocese to shoulder this obligation.[29]

The money needed by the Church comes almost entirely from the benefactions of the faithful, living and departed—all to often from the latter. Every living has its endowment which provides a fixed income for the incumbent and which is usually quite insufficient for the purpose and has to be supplemented.[30] All glebe land which was previously attached to a living is now vested in the diocese and is managed for the benefit of the diocesan stipends fund.[31] At one time tithe provided an important part of the income of incumbents and is the one exception to the statement that all the Church's money comes from benefactions, for it was in essence a tax on the proceeds of the land in the district. But it has now been virtually abolished.

[25.] e.g in Halsbury, vol. 14.
[26.] Episcopal Endowments and Stipends Measure, 1943 (No.2) and Cathedrals Measure, 1963 (No.2).
[27.] See p.108 *post.*
[28.] Parsonages Measure, 1938 (No.3).
[29.] Repair of Benefice Buildings Measure, 1972 (No.2).
[30.] See *infra.*
[31.] Endowments and Glebe Measure, 1976 (No.4).

This took place in stages, the final stage being that provided by the Tithe Act, 1936[32] (as amended by the Tithe Act, 1951),[33] whereby the owner of land subject to tithe no longer pays tithe, but instead pays to the Crown a redemption-annuity which will extinguish his liability by 1996, and the Crown in exchange has given redemption-stock to the former owner of the tithe. A further comparatively small source of income is provided by fees paid in respect of special services rendered, such as marriage fees and burial fees, now regulated by Tables of Fees laid down by statutory authority.[34] In many dioceses, however, the incumbent is under an obligation to make a return of the fees received by him and the augmentation, if any, paid to him by the diocese is reduced *pro tanto*.

But none of these sources of income is anything like sufficient for the Church's needs, and supplementation is provided in the main from two sources, namely the funds of the Church Commissioners and the gifts of the faithful, usually through collections in church or covenanted subscriptions.[35]

The Church Commissioners are the successors to the Ecclesiastical Commissioners and Queen Anne's Bounty.

The latter was the creation of that pious Sovereign whose conscience pricked her when she discovered that certain taxes levied *on* churchmen and formerly payable to the pope were enriching the royal coffers. The whole of the first year's profits of a spiritual preferment (known as first fruits) and thereafter a tenth part of the yearly profit of a living went before the Reformation to the pope. At the Reformation they were diverted to the Crown.[36] Queen Anne established her Bounty 'for the augmentation and maintenance of the poor clergy' and made over all these profits for that purpose.[37] The fund was

---

[32] 26 Geo. V and 1 Edw. VIII, c.43.

[33] 14 & 15 Geo. V, c.12.

[34] Ecclesiastical Fees Measure, 1962 (10 & 11 Eliz. II No. 1)

[35] Alms taken at the offertory are at the disposal of the minister and churchwardens for pious and charitable uses, wherein, if they cannot agree, the direction of the ordinary must be taken (rubric in Book of Common Prayer). Other collections are for such purposes as the minister and Parochial Church Council may decide. Collections taken by the minister other than in church are at his disposal. Of course, money may be devoted to any object other than that for which it was collected. See s.7 Parochial Church Councils (Powers) Measure, 1956 (No.5).

[36] Appointment of Bishops Act, 1533 (25 Hen. VIII, c.20) and First Fruits and Tenths Act, 1534 (26 Hen. VIII, c.3).

[37] Queen Anne's Bounty Act, 1703 (2 & 3 Anne, c.20).

further swollen by moneys from other sources. First fruits and tenths were abolished in 1926.[38] The Bounty, however, continued to function until its amalgamation with the Ecclesiastical Commissioners in 1948.[39]

The Ecclesiastical Commissioners were created by the Ecclesiastical Commissioners Act, 1836,[40] and their powers and composition widened by subsequent statutory enactments.[41] Their functions were both administrative and financial. In respect of the latter much Church property has been vested in them. The estates of sees and of cathedrals and of many ecclesiastical corporations and of suspended offices and sinecures were transferred to the Commissioners for redistribution for pastoral purposes, and it is out of the funds thus produced that many payments to the clergy are made and by which many inadequate endowments are supplemented.

In 1948, by the Church Commissioners Measure, 1947,[42] Queen Anne's Bounty and the Ecclesiastical Commissioners were merged into one body under the new title of Church Commissioners.

The two archbishops, all the diocesan bishops, the Lord Chancellor, the Speaker of the House of Commons, the Prime Minister, and many other holders of important offices are *ex officio* Commissioners, together with a large number of other persons both clerical and lay, appointed in a variety of ways. There are in addition three Commissioners known as Church Estates Commissioners, the First and Second being appointed by the Crown and the Third by the Archbishop of Canterbury. Of these, the First Estates Commissioner is in effect the acting head of most of the Commission's daily workings, assisted by the Third Estates Commissioner, while the Second is in practice always a member of the House of Commons, where he answers for the Commissioners. The Commissioners work under an elaborate constitution and have an expert staff, the main burden of the financial work falling upon the three Estates Commissioners.

[38.] First Fruits and Tenths Measure, 1926 (16 & 17 Geo. V, No.5).
[39.] Church Commissioners Measure, 1947 (10 & 11 Geo. VI, No. 2).
[40.] 6 & 7 Will. IV, c.77.
[41.] Ecclesiastical Commissioners Act of 1840 (3 & 4 Vict., c.113); 1850 (13 & 14 Vict., c.14); 1860 (23 & 24 Vict. c.124); 1875 (38 & 39 Vict., c.71), and many other Acts.
[42.] No. 2.

Among the many administrative functions which the Church Commissioners discharge in addition to looking after the finances entrusted to them are those connected with the formation of new parishes, the union of benefices, the alteration of the boundaries of parishes, and the making of schemes under the Pastoral Measure 1983.[43]

The contributions of the faithful, are, of course, often allocated to specific purposes ranging over a wide field of the Church's activities. Often much goes every week towards the expenses of the particular church where the collection is made; sometimes (but not sufficiently often) the parishioners undertake the burden of some of the parson's running expenses, such as telephone, postage, petrol and secretarial assistance; the whole or part of the stipend of an assistant curate is often provided by the parishioners; while the work of the Church overseas and many other charitable or religious objects are financed both by private donations and subscriptions and by collections in church. In each diocese there is also a system of voluntary taxation, often known as the diocesan quota, whereby each parish church is assessed for an annual contribution to diocesan funds. The dioceses are in turn assessed for an annual contribution to the funds administered on behalf of the Church Assembly by its Central Board of Finance. It is out of these moneys that the work of the Church Assembly through its many boards and committees[44] is largely financed. It is, too, out of the diocesan quota, together with other funds which the diocese may have collected, that supplementation of endowments is provided to bring the stipend of every incumbent up to the minimum fixed by that diocese, the diocese itself receiving a contribution from the Church Commissioners for this purpose. Until recently it was customary for the Easter offerings to be given to the incumbent. But today this seldom happens, since such offerings merely result in a *pro tanto* reduction in the augmentation paid by the diocese to the incumbent.

[43] No. 1.

[44] e.g. A.C.C.M. (the Advisory Council for the Church's Ministry), formerly C.A.C.T.M. (the Central Advisory Council for the Ministry), concerned with the recruitment and training, and, where necessary, the financing of ordinands; the Boards for Social Responsibility, concerned with, among other things, social welfare work; the Legal Board; and the Church Information Board.

The foregoing provides a very sketchy outline of a complicated subject, involving sums of money which are large, but yet inadequate, for their purpose. Two further points are worth noting briefly.

Whereas the secular courts of the land are maintained mainly out of taxation, the ecclesiastical courts of the land, together with their judges and officers, are inadequately maintained (as were all courts once) by a system of fees paid by the suitors.

Places used for public worship, together with church halls and other buildings ancillary to public worship, are exempt from rates.[45] This exemption is, of course, a hidden asset of considerable value.[46]

---

[45] Rating and Valuation (Miscellaneous Provisions) Act, 1955 (4 & 5 Eliz. II, c.9). The exemption is not confined to buildings of the Established Church and it is in danger of being lost if the building is let for other purposes.

[46] For an interesting and unexpected extension of this principle (in Scotland) see *Glasgow City Corporation's v. Johnstone and Others* (1963), 1 All E.R.. 730.

XII

CEREMONIAL, FURNISHINGS, AND DECORATIONS

It may seem odd that a chapter should be devoted to the law concerning ceremonial, furnishings, and decorations. But a whole volume would not be too long to contain an adequate review of the law on these subjects, for they have aroused the strongest feelings and have given rise to much litigation and a wealth of reported cases, many of them containing a good deal of bad law. The reason for this spate of litigation is partly, but not wholly, a capacity on the part of churchmen (and others) to get deeply concerned about trivialities. It is also due in part to the fact that matters of profounder theological import are often enshrined in outward forms and observances. But the root cause is that the Church of England embraces in one fold churchmen of widely differing outlooks, and in the seventeenth century she sought to maintain this precarious yet long-lasting embrace by an attempt to impose an impossibly rigid code of uniformity. At the best of times such a rigid code would have been impractical; but the contemporaneous occurrence of the Oxford Movement and the evangelical revival in the nineteenth century produced an added tension which caused eruptions into the courts of law, unfortunately at a time when the judges were not best fitted for work in this particular field. Today we are beginning to view these controversies from a more detached standpoint and in a better perspective. We can now recognize that the High Church party did valuable work in reminding us of our Catholic heritage and in restoring dignity and beauty to our worship. It is not surprising that at times its members indulged in excesses and were sometimes tactless and provocative. But the Low Church party was often too easily provoked, and certainly had failed to appreciate that the Anglican formularies were carefully designed to satisfy Protestantism while also embracing Catholicism. Since the judges were for the most part far from High and were often deficient in liturgical and theological scholarship, the Low Church party won a number of minor and sometimes undeserved victories at first, which, together with some inconsistent decisions, have resulted in a degree of embarrassment today which in turn has often resulted in a tacit agreement on all sides to ignore the law entirely. In these circumstances this chapter will deal only in barest outline with the subject, leaving the reader who wishes to make more extensive researches to pursue them in other works.[1] It will be found that reference has already been made elsewhere[2] to some of the matters mentioned here.

The Act of Uniformity, 1662,[3] together with the rubrics in the Book of Common Prayer annexed thereto, and especially the Ornaments rubric, undoubtedly provide a code of considerable rigidity, aimed at promoting a universal practice in the conduct of public worship. It has been argued elsewhere[4] that the code is not so rigid as has sometimes been thought, but rigid it certainly is. It is thus at lease *prima facie* an offence in public worship to add to or subtract from anything in the Prayer Book, whether by way of words or ceremonial, and any furnishings of the church designed to assist such deviations are, therefore prima facie unlawful. The introduction of other authorized forms of service, the doctrine of necessity, the *jus liturgicum*, and the fact that the rubrics in the Prayer Book should be construed as directives rather than as sections in an Act of Parliament[5] may have an important bearing on whether something is lawful or unlawful, but one's starting-point is, nevertheless, what the rubrics plainly say. The unfortunate tendency of the courts in the nineteenth century to construe the rubrics as they would construe Acts of Parliament led to a rigidity which may now be softened by the provisions in the new Ecclesiastical Jurisdiction Measure, 1963,[6] that the Commission of Review and the Court of Ecclesiastical Causes Reserved[7] shall not be bound by the decisions of the Judicial Committee of the Privy Council; but, though these decisions are no longer binding on those two tribunals, they cannot be wholly ignored.

[1.] e.g. Halsbury, vol. 14 especially the cases cited in paras 953-971, (inclusive).
[2.] e.g. in Chapter VII *ante*.
[3.] 14 Car. II, c. 4.
[4.] See pp.68–70 *ante*.
[5.] See pp.59–60 *ante*.
[6.] No. 1, s.45(3) and s.48(5).
[7.] See Chapter XIV *post*.

A good deal of argument has turned on what is and what is not to be regarded as a ceremony. Thus, the legality of a procession has even been questioned.[8] It is clear that the ministers (including in that term servers and singers) must go into church and come out again, and, if they choose to do so together and in an orderly fashion, this would seem to be a procession, and it is difficult to see how such a procession can possibly be described as unlawful, especially since it occurs before or after, rather than during, a service;[9] but to go in procession during a service from a given point back to a given point might well be described as a ceremony and, if not explicitly or implicitly authorized or directed by the Prayer Book or other lawful form of service,[10] could be at least vulnerable on the score of legality.

It is not intended here to give an exhaustive account of all the minutiae about which there has been litigation. One of the most fruitful sources of dispute has been as to the position, actions, and posture of the priest at the celebration of the Holy Communion[11] and as to the legality or otherwise of Reservation.[12] The decisions leave it by no means clear how far the courts think that the priest is confined within a rigid code as to his movements.

The chaotic position in which the reported decisions of the nineteenth century might land us, if they were all taken seriously, can be shown by some almost random examples. It would seem that it is lawful to sing hymns, although no place for them is to be found in the Prayer Book.[13] On the strength of this, the archbishops came to the conclusion (sensibly, but not necessarily correctly) that to sing or say 'Glory be to thee, O God' at the reading of the Gospel and to sing the *Agnus Dei* after the prayer of consecration is lawful.[14] But to give notice during

8.   *Elphinstone v. Purchas*, [1870] L.R. 3 A. and E. 66.
9.   *Read v. Bishop of Lincoln* (1892), A.C. 644 P.C.
10.   *Re St. Peter and St. Paul, Leckhampton* (1967) 3 All E.R. 1057.
11.   See Halsbury, vol. 14 paras 983-984 and the cases there cited. In *Martin* v. *Mackonochie*, [1868] L.R. 2 A. and E. 116, it was held, rightly or wrongly, that it was an offence to elevate the consecrated elements above the head, and the defendant was admonished not to do so again. Thereafter he elevated them only to the level of the head. In *Martin v. Mackonochie*, [1869], L.R. 3 P.C. 52, it was held that he had not thereby broken the monition. It was not held, as is often supposed, that it is lawful to elevate the elements only as far as the head.
12.   See pp.79 and 96 *ante*.
13.   *Read v. Bishop of Lincoln, supra*.

divine worship of the feasts of St. Leonard, St. Martin, or St. Britius (which are not mentioned as holy days in the Prayer Book) has been said to be unlawful,[15] from which (if it is right) it would seem to follow that it would also be unlawful to give notice of a forthcoming church fete. The use of incense during a statutory service is probably unlawful, but, if sanctioned by the bishop in the exercise of the *jus liturgicum*, may perhaps be lawful during other services.[16] The ringing of a bell, however, at the prayer of consecration appears to be unlawful,[17] though why this should be so, while the singing of the *Agnus Dei* is lawful (if it is), passes all reasonable comprehension.

It will be realized from this that any modification in public worship, however slight, is introduced at the minister's peril. The peril is not great, as proceedings are today unlikely to be taken against him; but in the last century they were real. The situation has now been eased by the passing of the Church of England (Worship and Doctrine) measure 1974.[18] Canon B4 also specifically authorizes the Convocations, the archbishops and the ordinary to make provision for occasions for which the Prayer Book or the General Synod makes no provision, and Canon B5 even permits the minister, subject to Convocation, to do the same, and, on his own authority, to make variations which are not of substantial importance. It remains to be seen how this Measure will work in practice. It may be that the provision made by it for lawful variation will have the effect of curbing the almost universal liberty enjoyed in practice for so long whereby each minister unlawfully made such variations as he himself found pleasing. Parish priests may now find that they have exchanged a wide measure of illegal freedom for a narrow one of authorized, but closely supervised, experiment.

From the close control which the Act of Uniformity and judicial decisions have sought to impose in matters of ceremonial there has naturally flowed a close control of ceremonial's ancillaries, furnishings,[19] and decorations. With regard to these it is necessary to distinguish, on the one hand, the ornaments of the church from those of the ministers, and, on

[14.] Lambeth Opinions on Incense and Processional Lights (July 1899).
[15.] *Elphinstone v. Purchas, supra.*
[16.] *Re St. Mary's, Tyne Dock* (1954) 2 All E.R. 339.   [17.] Ibid.
[18.] No. 3. See p.67 *ante.*
[19.] But not books, save for those in parochial libraries, for which see p.134 *post.*

the other hand, in the former case, to distinguish between what are technically called ornaments and those accessories which are not technically called ornaments.

With regard to the furnishings of the church, the term *ornament* is confined to those things which are used in or about the services of the church. Thus, the holy table, the font, the Communion vessels, the bell, the Bible, and the Prayer Book are all ornaments.[20] It would seem, on this definition, that many other things are also ornaments, such as pews, the credence table, and hassocks. But crosses, flower vases, and stained-glass windows are not ornaments in this technical sense. The notorious Ornaments rubric immediately before the Order for the Morning Prayer in the Prayer Book states 'that such Ornaments of the Church, and of the Ministers thereof at all times of their Ministration, shall be retained, and be in use, as were in this Church of England by the Authority of Parliament, in the Second Year of the Reign of King *Edward* the Sixth'. There has been read into this rubric an implication that any ornament which was not so in use is not to be retained, and from this there has followed prolonged and inconclusive argument both as to what period is meant by 'the Second Year of the Reign of King *Edward* the Sixth', and also as to what ornaments were then in use 'by the Authority of Parliament'. But, so far as the ornaments of the church are concerned (as distinct from the ornaments of the ministers), the courts have been more concerned with the use to which an ornament is put than with the question of whether it was in use with Parliament's authority at a particular date. The rubric is mandatory about what must be retained (the holy table, Bible, Prayer Book, Communion vessels, and bell, at the least); but about these there has been comparatively little dispute. It is concerning the introduction of other ornaments that dispute has arisen, and, in general, the courts have tended to take the line that an ornament is not unlawful if the use to which it is to be put is consistent with lawful ceremonial, but that it is unlawful if it is to be used for unlawful ceremonial. Thus, organs,[21]

---

[20]   A box to receive alms for the poor is enjoyed by Canon F10. It would seem to be an ornament, though not directly used in worship.

[21]   *Westerton v. Liddell* (1855), Moore's Special Report. For so-called electric organs, see *Re St Mary's, Lancaster* (1980) 1 W.L.R. 657.

pews, hassocks, and bookcases are all undoubtedly lawful (whether or not they be ornaments), for the use of all of them is consistent with lawful worship. Church bells are also lawful.[22] But a sanctus bell or gong[23] has been held to be unlawful, because the ringing of it at the prayer of consecration has (however dubiously) been held to be an unlawful ceremony. The same considerations apply to the ancillaries to Reservation. If Reservation be lawful, an aumbry is also lawful; but, if Reservation be unlawful, any facility designed exclusively for that purpose is unlawful.[24] Similarly, a thurible may be lawful, since some uses of incense are lawful; but, if the use to which it is to be put is for an unlawful ceremony, a faculty will not be granted.[25]

If an ornament is unlawful, no faculty for its introduction can properly be granted. If, however, an ornament is lawful, it is a matter of discretion whether or not it should be granted, and, if the chancellor is of the opinion that it is likely to be used for an unlawful purpose, he may refuse a faculty even though in itself the ornament is lawful.[26]

Canon F2 makes provision for the altar or holy table, which is to be 'covered, in time of Divine Service, with a covering of silk or other decent stuff, and with a fair white linen cloth at the time of the celebration of the Holy Communion. Canon 82 of 1603 clearly envisaged that the altar should be movable, and it was the custom in the seventeenth century to move it into the body of the church for a celebration, placing it longwise, with the narrow ends at the liturgical east and west (hence the origin of the custom, at one time prevalent, of the minister's standing at the north side, which, being a long side, was a convenient position). From the idea that the altar should be movable there sprang the further idea that it should be made of wood and not

---

[22] Canon F8 requires there to be 'at least one bell' in every church or chapel.

[23] *Re St. Mary's Tyne Dock* (1954), 2 All E.R. 339.

[24] For Reservation, see pp. 79 and 96 *ante*.

[25] *Re St. Mary's, Tyne Dock* (1954), 2 All E.R. 339.

[26] For a baldachino, see *Re St. Nicholas, Plumstead* (1961), 1 All E.R. 298; for a ciborium, see *Re St. Mary's, Tyne Dock*, supra; for a pyx, see *Re St. Nicholas, Plumstead, supra*; for sanctuary lamps, see *Re All Saints, Leamington Priors (1963)*, 2 All E.R. 1062; for a place for hearing confessions, *see Re St. Mary's, Tyne Dock, supra*; and, in all instances, the cases therein cited. For faculties generally, see Chapter XIV *post*.

of stone,[27] at any rate if it was the principal altar. But legal controversy (though not necessarily liturgical controversy) has now been silenced by the Holy Table Measure, 1964,[28] which enacts that any suitable material may be used and that the table may be movable or immovable.[29]

When one turns from ornaments to decorations, one finds much the same reasoning. The legality of an ornament depends in the main upon the legality of the use to which it is to be put. The legality or, at least, the propriety of a decoration usually depends on whether it is or is not likely to give rise to 'superstitious reverence'[30] or to inculcate true or erroneous doctrine. Among the decorations which have been considered by the courts (some of them again and again) are crosses, crucifixes, statues, windows, reredoses, chancel screens, roods, and stations of the cross. Each of these has at times been allowed and at times refused, according to times and circumstances, and from these decisions[31] the principle just enunciated seems to emerge, albeit a little shakily. Memorial tablets (technically *decorations*, but often far from decorative) have given rise to dispute when the inscription has invited prayers for the dead, though it has several times been held[32] that such prayers are not contrary to the doctrine of the Church of England. Flower vases seem almost to have succeeded in keeping out of theological controversy,[33] all too frequently compensating for their liturgical innocuousness by their brazen aesthetic aggressiveness. Candles, however, have excited emotions fairly

---

27. But see *Re St. John the Divine, Richmond* (1953), 1 All E.R. 818.

28. No. 4. Now repealed; but similar provision is made in Canon F2.

29. Immobility has thus become lawful just at the moment when (pace the observation in *Re St. John the Divine, Richmond,* supra) a tendency to move the altar and take the westward-facing position has manifested itself.

30. The expression was used by Lord Penzance in *Clifton v. Ridsdale* (1876), 1 P.D. 316. For a comment on these words see *Re St. Peter, St. Helier, Morden; Re St. Olave, Mitcham* (1951), 2 All E.R. 53. *See also Re St. Edward the Confessor, Mottingham* (1983) 1 W.L.R. 364.

31. For the decided cases see Halsbury, vol. 14, paras 960-969, and also the digests of cases for those since 1975.

32. e.g. in *Re St. Mary the Virgin, Ilmington* (1962), 1 All E.R. 560. The arguments are bound up with views concerning Purgatory. It is to be noted that Article XXII of the Thirty-nine Articles does not condemn the doctrine of Purgatory, but only the Romish doctrine of Purgatory.

33. Almost, but not quite, for even they were caught by *Elphinstone v. Purchas* [1870], L.R. 3 A. and E. 66.

often. There is clear nothing intrinsically unlawful in a candle, the main purpose of most candles being to give light. But the ceremonial use of candles has been said to be unlawful,[34] and, therefore, perhaps the matter should be regarded as one of ceremony rather than as one of ornaments or decorations. But the decorative use of candles at the altar is nevertheless permissible and the number so used is within the discretion of the court.[35]

Among the embellishments which are often to be found in churches are heraldic devices. These are valued both for their decorative qualities and also for their significance. In particular, the royal arms are displayed in many churches. When a faculty is sought for the introduction of such devices, the duty of the court varies according to whether they are wanted solely as decoration or also for their significance. If they are wanted solely for decoration, the court must be satisfied that no reasonable objection to their use as such can be made by the person entitled to the emblems, for he has a proprietary interest in them.[36] But, in the case of the royal arms, where their introduction is wanted in order to signify the Royal Supremacy, it would seem unlikely that, so long as that supremacy is claimed, any objection by the Crown to their use could be sustained.[37] The same considerations apply to the arms of the diocese or of the province or to the use of St. George's Cross as signifying England.[38]

---

[34]   *Sumner v. Wise,* [1870] L.R. 3 A. and E. 58; *Elphinstone v. Purchas,* [1870] L.R. 3 A. and E. 66 and [1871] L.R. 3 P.C. 605 (sub-nom. *Hebbert v. Purchas*); *Martin v. Mackonochie,* [1868] L.R. 2 P.C. 365; *Read v. Bishop of Lincoln* (1892), A.C. 644 P.C.; *Rector and Churchwardens of Capel St.* Mary v. *Packard* (1927), P. 289.

[35]   *Re Holy Trinity, Woolwich* (1949), P. 369; *Re St. Saviour's, Walthamstow* (1951), P.147; *Re St. George's, Southall (1952), 1 All E.R. 323.* The use of electric lights designed in imitation of candles has been disapproved; *Re St. Andrew's Dearley* (1981) Fam. 50.

[36]   *Manchester Corporation v. Manchester Palace of Variety Ltd.* (Court of Chivalry) (1955), 1 All E.R. 387.

[37]   *Re West Tarring Parish Church* (1954), 2 All E.R. 591; *Re St. Paul, Battersea* (1954), 2 All E.R. 595.

[38]   The claim sometimes advanced by admirals that they have an exclusive proprietary interest in the flag of St. George is clearly not to be entertained. The army, not for the first time, has shown greater modesty; for it has never been claimed that a Commander-in-Chief has an exclusive interest in the Union flag. The custom is growing of churches' flying a flag consisting of St. George's Cross, the whole being differenced by the addition of the arms of the diocese.

While the ornaments and the decorations of the church have been the source of much controversy, the ornaments of the ministers have by no means escaped. In this context *ornaments* means the things which the ministers put on, such as robes, headgear, rings, and crosses, while *minister* is a term wide enough to include clergymen, servers, singers, and vergers.

The Canons of 1603 (now replaced) showed considerable concern for the apparel of ordained ministers, Canon 74 dealing with what they should wear out of church, and even in bed, or at least in the home.[39] It need scarcely be said that what is still the most common mark of the cleric (though beginning to disappear), the clerical collar, commonly known as a dog-collar or Roman collar, being an unpleasant and continental innovation of the nineteenth century, finds no mention in the Canons of 1603 or in any other official regulation.

Canons 24, 25, and 58 of 1603 dealt with the clothes to be worn in church. No mention, however, was made of that most common of all ecclesiastical garments, the cassock, and perhaps it was tacitly assumed that this should be the foundation upon which the rest is to be based. And, for the rest, the Canons appear to have opted heavily for the garment most closely associated with the abuses which the Reformation was seeking to combat, namely, the medieval surplice, rather than the more primitive vestments. The surplice, with, in the case of graduates, the appropriate hood, and, in the case of non-graduates, an optional 'decent Tippet of black, so it be not silk', was the dress for divine service, be it the Holy Communion or Matins, Evensong, or some other office, a cope being directed for 'the Principal Minister' at the Holy Communion in cathedral and collegiate churches. There was no mention of the black scarf which today is normally worn with the surplice and hood. It is possible that the black tippet for non-graduates is the scarf; but for graduates it would seem that the hood alone was the only accompaniment of the surplice envisaged by the Canons. But canons give way before Acts of Parliament, and, therefore, after 1662, the Canons had to be read subject to the Ornaments rubric in the Book of Common Prayer which had

---

[39]   See now Canon C27.

the authority of that Act.[40] With the Tractarian Movement in the nineteenth century, controversy, therefore, revolved around the question of what ornaments were in use, as the rubric has it, 'by the Authority of Parliament, in the Second Year of the Reign of King *Edward* the Sixth'. The surplice for Matins and Evensong was universally recognized as correct; but should it be the surplice or the eucharistic vestments for Holy Communion? Happily we need no longer pursue this fierce controversy, for the unresolved argument has now been outdated by the Vesture of Ministers Measure, 1964,[41] and Canon B8 which replaced it. This achieves a hard-fought compromise by seeking to legalize every form of usage, lawful or unlawful, current in the Church of England. It even mentions the cassock and scarf. For Morning and Evening prayer the minister is to wear cassock, surplice, and scarf. For the occasional offices he is to wear cassock, surplice, and scarf or stole. He may, if so entitled, wear a hood with his scarf. For Holy Communion, in addition to the cassock, the celebrant, the gospeller, and the epistoler may wear either the alb and customary vestments,[42] or surplice and stole, or surplice and scarf, with or without a hood, or alb and stole. Copes may be worn 'on any appropriate occasion'. In a parish church, however, whatever is customary is not to be altered without the consent of the Parochial Church Council, though in the case of disagreement between the minister and the Council the directions of the bishop are to be taken. No mention is made concerning headgear; but the use of a biretta for purposes of protection (or of a skull-cap) is lawful, though otherwise its legality is doubtful.[43] Black preaching gowns have the authority of long usage,[44] but seem to have been overlooked by the Measure, and, therefore, have possibly become unlawful *per incuriam* at Morning or Evening Prayer or Holy Communion, though no doubt lawful at other times.

[40]   14 Car. II, c.4.

[41]   No. 7.

[42]   Chasuble, tunicle, dalmatic, amice, maniple, and stole.

[43]   *Elphinstone v. Purchas*, [1870] L.R. 3 A. and E. 66 and [1871] L.R. 3 P.C. 605 (sub-nom. *Hebbert v. Purchas*)

[44]   *Re Robinson, Wright v. Tugwell* (1897), 1 Ch. 85, C.A.

The dress of bishops has not been the subject of litigation or legislation. It would seem that copes, mitres, rings and pectoral crosses are lawful and right on the appropriate occasions. The familiar 'magpie' of rochet and black chimere (with black wristbands) is regarded as the choir-habit, and presumably there is nothing wrong in wearing Convocation robes (scarlet chimere and wristbands) in choir, though there is not much to be said for the frequency with which some bishops discard the magpie for the scarlet. At the altar, however, an ordinary alb with uncrossed stole (with or without vestments) is clearly more appropriate than choir-habit. The many shades of episcopal purple for the cassock, making a platform-full of bishops look 'just like a bed of petunias',[45] have no warranty other than custom, but are clearly lawful. Indeed, there is no rule regarding the colour of cassocks for anyone, though scarlet by custom should be reserved to royal chaplains and members of royal foundations.

In the conduct of public worship a reader should wear cassock, surplice, the hood of his degree and (usually) a blue scarf. Servers, choristers, and others have been free from the dictates of the law in the matter of their clothing, which depends on the liturgical knowledge and taste (or lack of them) of those responsible in each particular case. Even a choir of women resplendent in floppy caps and purple, like so many bishopesses, is neither enjoined nor forbidden by the law and, in these days of ecumenism, might even be defended on the ground that it provides something in common with Congregationalism.[46]

[45.] Attributed to Bishop Montgomery-Campbell.
[46.] *Vide* the City Temple.

XIII

ECCLESIASTICAL PERSONS

In a sense, every member of the laos, God's people, is an ecclesiastical person, having been admitted into the family of God and to the membership of his Church at baptism.

Now there are diversities of gifts, but the same spirit. And there are differences of administrations, but the same Lord. And there are diversities of operations, but it is the same God which worketh all in all. . . . For by one Spirit we are all baptized into one body. . . . For the body is not one member, but many. . . . If the whole body were an eye, where were hearing? If the whole were hearing, where were the smelling? But now God hath set the members every one of them in the body, as it hath pleased him. And if they were all one member, where were the body? But now are they many members, yet but one body.[1]

The task of the entire laos is, as the Body of Christ on earth, to continue here the ministry of Our Lord, in constant communion with God, in the offering of worship and prayer and thanksgiving, and in seeking to bring souls to God by going out into all the world and preaching the Gospel by word and deed, sacrificially showing forth the divine compassion.

But, within this total activity of the whole body, to each member is allotted his or her own peculiar task, and some of the functions fall naturally to different categories of persons. It is with these categories that we are here concerned, in so far as the law has differentiated between them.

Within the total laos the sharpest distinction has tended to come between the clergy and those called laity (that is, in common parlance, those members of the laos who are not clergymen). The sharpness of the distinction has varied from time to time and from place to place. In England it was in some respects less sharp before the Reformation than afterwards. The existence of many in minor orders (doorkeepers, readers, exorcists, and acolytes, and, before 1207, subdeacons), who

---

[1.] I Corinthians xii.

might proceed to major orders (deacon, priest, and bishop) or might revert to completely secular status, helped to blur the clergy-line[2] as did also the religious (monks, friars, and nuns), who, among the men, sometimes were and sometimes were not ordained. At a time when learning was confined to a few who were closely connected with the work of the Church, it was natural to find any post requiring learning filled by a 'clerk', ordained or unordained, however secular the actual job might be. Thus lawyers, civil servants (as we would now call them), Ministers of the Crown, and teachers were likely to be clerks, while the lay brothers[3] in the religious orders spent much of their time on work in the kitchens and on the farms. To this must be added benefit of clergy, eventually accorded to all men who could make a show of reading (and to nuns), and granting them a limited exemption from the criminal jurisdiction of the secular courts—a privilege and an abuse which was not wholly abolished until 1827.[4]

After the Reformation, by which time learning had become more general and secular posts requiring learning could be filled by laymen, the tendency for many years was to regard the sacred ministers as persons set apart who should devote their whole time to so-called sacred matters. Teaching and farming were regarded as appropriate occupations for them, but other secular occupations were more dubious. The twentieth century has seen a swing of opinion in the other direction and there has sprouted the idea that the 'involvement' of the clergy in the affairs of the world is somehow a logical consequence of the Incarnation. This found its most spectacular expression in the 'priest-worker' movement in France; but it has by no means been ignored in England. Not only are some priests to be found in secular jobs, but there has also been a movement towards 'clericalizing' the laity. This movement has received an added

---

2. Reginald Pole was Dean of Wimborne, Dean of Exeter, Prebendary of Biscombe, and Prebendary of Yatminster Secunda and was offered the Bishopric of Winchester and the Archbishopric of York while not even a deacon. He was made deacon only in order to become a Cardinal and was not priested or consecrated until he had accepted the Archbishopric of Canterbury.

3. Not to be confused with unordained choir-monks.

4. The Criminal Law Act, 1827 (7 & 8 Geo. IV, c. 28). In South Carolina in the United States benefit was successfully claimed as late as 1855 in *The State* v. *Bosse* (1855), 42 S.C. 276.

impetus from the fact that there are not enough clergymen to do all the work required of them, and it was thought in some quarters that their labours might be supplemented if some who at present are laymen were to be ordained without relinquishing their secular occupations. Over the past 10 or so years this tendency has found expression in the ordination of a very considerable number of laymen into what has become known as the non-stipendiary ministry. Such men first undergo a course of theological training and, after ordination, usually continue in their secular occupations, though often while also giving clerical assistance in some parish. Sometimes, after a time, they leave their secular occupation and take some purely clerical office in all respects like any man ordained to the ministry after more traditional training.

Canon C26 nonetheless enacts that 'A minister shall not give himself to such occupations, habits, or recreations as do not befit his sacred calling, or may be detrimental to the performance of the duties of his office, or tend to be a just cause of offence to others! Furthermore, by Canon C28 'No minister holding ecclesiastical office shall engage in trade or any other occupation in such manner as to affect the performance of the duties of his office', save under statutory authority or with the licence of his bishop (who is bound to consult with the Parochial Church Council). The minister may appeal against the refusal of a licence to the archbishop. The Pluralities Act, 1838,[5] strengthens these canons by forbidding any spiritual person who holds any cathedral preferment or benefice or curacy or lectureship or who is licensed or allowed to perform the duties of any ecclesiastical office to farm more than eighty acres of land without the permission of the bishop, or to engage in trade. The Act[6] makes exceptions with regard to teaching, the buying and selling of household or personal goods, and in respect of other minor matters. Since these exceptions are statutory no episcopal licence is needed under Canon C28. In considering these direct prohibitions, moreover, attention must also be paid to direct injunctions, such as the rubric in the Prayer Book directing all priests and deacons to say Morning and Evening prayer daily,

[5.] 1 & 2 Vict., c. 106, ss. 28 and 29. See also the Trading Partnership Act, 1841 (4 & 5 Vict., c. 14).

[6.] S. 30.

if not publicly then privately.[7] To these must be added the words laid down in the Ordinal for the bishop to address to the ordinands, namely, 'Ye ought to forsake and set aside (as much as you may) all worldly cares and studies. We have good hope . . . that you have clearly determined . . . to give yourselves wholly to this office . . . so that, as much as lieth in you, you will apply yourselves wholly to this one thing, and draw all your cares and studies this way. . . .'

Since every bishop is also a priest and a deacon, these restrictions apply equally to them. A diocesan bishop, however, may *ex officio* have a seat in the House of Lords,[8] but an episcopally ordained priest or deacon, whether of the Established Church or of any other Church except the Church in Wales, is forbidden to sit in the House of Commons,[9] though they are not forbidden to be members of local authorities,[10] nor, if they be peers in their own right, are they forbidden to sit in the House of Lords.

The Clerical Disabilities Act, 1870[11] permits the relinquishment of holy orders by deed, though not so as to avoid the consequences of any pending legal proceedings. The effect of such a deed is to relieve the person executing it from all the disabilities attaching to his order and to deprive him of all its privileges, so that he becomes for all practical purposes a layman again. But, since his orders are indelible,[12] he does not cease to be an ordained man, and he may petition the archbishop of the province wherein his deed is recorded, and, if the archbishop agrees, the enrolment of the deed is vacated and he becomes once again for all purposes an ordained person without any further ordination (for such, indeed, is theologically impossible).

[7] At the end of the article entitled 'Concerning the services of the Church'. See also Canon C26.
[8] See Chapter III *ante*.
[9] House of Commons (Clergy Disqualification) Act, 1801 (41 Geo. III, c.63). For other episcopally ordained ministers, see *Re MacManaway* (1951), A.C. 161 P.C. For Wales, see Welsh Church Act., 1914 (4 & 5 Geo. V, c. 91).
[10] Ministers of Religion (Removal of Disqualification) Act, 1925 (15 & 16 Geo. V, c. 54), repealed but in effect re-enacted by ss. 57 and 58 of the Local Government Act, 1933 (23 & 24 Geo. V, c. 51), itself now repealed. The current legislation (the Local Government Act 1972 (20 & 21 Eliz. II, c70)) simply omits the clergy from the list of persons disqualified; see s.80.
[11] 33 & 34 Vict., c. 91.
[12] See Canon C. 1.

The privileges enjoyed by the clergy are small. They are exempt from jury service.[13] They are privileged from arrest on civil (but not on criminal) process when going to or from Convocation (if they are members) or when going to or from an episcopal visitation; and beneficed property is exempt from sequestration except by the bishop.[14] They are specially protected while officiating at a burial or in a place of worship, and it is a special offence to interfere with them then.[15] They are usually exempted from being conscripted into the Armed Forces.[16]

While a deacon shares all the disabilities of the priest, his functions are limited by the Ordinal to assisting him in divine service and especially at the distribution of the Holy Communion (where his assistance may be with either the chalice or the paten), to reading the Scriptures and homilies in church and to instructing youth in the catechism, and (in the absence of the priest) to baptizing infants, and, (if licensed by the bishop), to preaching, and to searching out the sick, the poor, and the impotent. In practice he also frequently takes funerals, and, if he should officiate at a marriage, the marriage (which is essentially the act of the contracting parties) is almost certainly valid,[17] though canonically irregular, as a deacon is not commissioned to give the Blessing.

Though in law the clergy-line today is still drawn between the ordinary run of men and women on the one hand, and, on the other hand, the bishops, priests, and deacons (the orders which, so the Preface to the Ordinal optimistically states, it is evident to all men diligently reading Holy Scripture have existed since the Apostles' time), this neat dichotomy is in practice once again becoming a little untidy. Three matters in particular have contributed to this: the revival of the order of deaconesses, the revival of the order of readers, and the revival of religious orders.

[13.] Juries Act, 1974 (22 & 23 Eliz. II, c. 23).

[14.] See Halsbury, vol.14, paras 675 and 894 et seq.; *McGrath v. Geraghty* (1866) 15 W.R. 127; *Blane* v. *Geraghty*, ibid. 133.

[15.] Offences against the Person Act, 1861 (24 & 25 Vict., c. 100) and Criminal Justice Act, 1948 (11 & 12 Geo. VI, c. 58).

[16.] See e.g. National Service Act, 1948 (11 & 12 Geo. VI, c. 64), s. 1 and First Schedule.

[17.] R. v. *Millis* (1844) 10 Cl. and Fin. 534. See p.92 *ante*.

The Church today, as in all ages, leans heavily upon the ministry of women in innumerable ways. But her theology on the subject is confused and variable. For example, nobody is quite sure what the status of a deaconess is; but it is certain that, whereas a deacon is in law a clerk in holy orders, a deaconess in law is not.[18]

There are in practice two sorts of reader;[19] the diocesan reader and the parochial reader. They are commissioned by the bishop, after examination, to function respectively in either the diocese or in a particular parish. They in practice provide a supplementary ministry of the greatest value in preaching and taking such services as do not liturgically require a priest. Their exact status in law is, however, doubtful. The publication of banns by a reader is valid, because the Marriage Act, 1949,[20] says that banns may be published by a layman, and a reader, in law, is not a clerk in holy orders and is, therefore, a layman. They are frequently licensed by the bishop to assist at the distribution of the Holy Communion,[21] and may also be licensed to officiate at burials and cremations. The revival of this order, as well as being of great practical value, has led to a healthy, but so far inconclusive, theological reconsideration of the nature of the diaconate, for liturgically there is no difference in function today between a deacon and a reader.[22]

In the middle ages unease was caused by a tendency among some prelates to enlarge their following by the ordination of persons with no particular job to do. As a check to this tendency the Canon Law provided that in such cases the bishop himself was bound to provide for any person whom he ordained other than to an adequate title. An exception was made where the candidate for ordination was a Fellow of a College in Cambridge or Oxford or was a member of a religious order. Canon 23 of the Canons of 1603 (now repealed) re-enacted the pre-Reformation Canon Law, but, the monasteries having been dissolved, made no mention of members of religious orders. The revival in recent times of religious orders within the

---

[18.] See Canons D1, D2 and D3.
[19.] They are frequently, but unhappily, called *lay-readers*.
[20.] S. 9(2) (12, 13, & 14 Geo. VI, c. 76).
[21.] See Canons B12 and E4.
[22.] See also Canon E7 for the functions of other lay workers.

Church of England has been of immense value to the spiritual life of the Church, and bishops were in practice prepared to ordain the members of such orders 'to the title of Holy Poverty'. The position has to some extent now been regularized by Canon C5 which expressly permits the ordination of 'any person who is living under vows in the house of any religious order or community.' Whether this permission is sufficient to relieve a bishop of the obligation to maintain a religious whom he has ordained is not clear; but the chances of an action for maintenance against a bishop in such circumstances seem remote. In strict law religious houses are simply ordinary private houses, like any others within the parish and diocese. Their chapels, therefore, are caught by all the rules relating to private chapels.[23] Their members, if they be bishops or priests or deacons, are governed by the rules relevant to all the ordained. If a monk or friar is not ordained, he is in law a layman. He would thus be liable, as would a nun, to jury service, unless he can properly be described as 'a vowed member of any religious order living in a monastery, convent or other religious community'.[24] Difficulty is more likely to arise over conscription. So far the secular authorities have been prepared in practice to exempt the professed from service in the Armed Forces and the different orders have usually been willing that those not yet professed should do their national service. But the strict legal position will in each case depend upon the construction of whatever legislation is in force at the material time.[25] There are other persons who, in some special sense, are ecclesiastical persons. Among them are the Sovereign, chancellors, churchwardens, and sidesmen. But no further mention is made of them here, because either they have received attention elsewhere, or there is nothing in their status, as distinct from their office, which requires remark.

---

[23] See p.55 *ante.*

[24] Juries Act, 1974 (22 & 23 Eliz. II, c 23), Schedule 1.

[25] Willing as the State might be to exempt all religious from obligations to perform military service, the situation is complicated by the claims for exemption which, for example, Jehovah's Witnesses might advance and which the State might not be willing to concede.

XIV

ECCLESIASTICAL COURTS AND LEGAL PROCEEDINGS

1. GENERAL

As has already been observed,[1] because the Church of England is established, the Church's courts are courts of the State and the State's courts are courts of the Church. It may easily happen that the simplest way of enforcing ecclesiastical rights is by proceedings in one of the temporal courts. Thus, if someone were to be discovered manifestly about to lay drains under a churchyard without the authority of a faculty, it may well be that the quickest way to stop him would be by applying to the Chancery Division of the High Court for an injunction.

It often happens, therefore, that decisions on ecclesiastical law are given in the temporal courts and that points of ecclesiastical law are to be found in the reports of cases in the temporal courts whose judges in arriving at their conclusions have themselves had recourse to the reported decisions of the ecclesiastical courts. But, nevertheless, there are appropriate tribunals in England for all types of legal proceedings, and usually an ecclesiastical court is the appropriate tribunal for an ecclesiastical matter. The Church, therefore, has its own system of courts, both of first instance and appellate, running parallel to the temporal courts and neither inferior nor superior to them.[2]

Thus, no appeal lies from an ecclesiastical court to a secular court. An order in the nature of a writ of prohibition, however, may issue out of the Queen's Bench Division to restrain an ecclesiastical court from exceeding its jurisdiction. This is

---

[1.] Chapter II
[2.] See Halsbury, vol. II, tit. *Crown Proceedings*, esp. paras. 1521-1573; ibid. vol. 14, tit. *Ecclesiastical Law*, paras. 1267-1269; and *R. v. Chancellor of St. Edmundsbury and Ipswich Diocese ex parte White* (1948), 1 K.B. 195 and the cases there cited.

probably because, before the Reformation, the ecclesiastical courts were not the king's courts, and this writ provided one of the means by which attempts at papal usurpation were kept in check. Despite the fact that at the Reformation the ecclesiastical courts became the king's courts, there has been no diminution of this limited power of control by the Queen's Bench, and it is even thought that the order may be directed by the Queen's Bench to that most royal of tribunals, the Privy Council, when acting in its capacity as an appellate ecclesiastical court.[3] If this be so, the order may also presumably be directed to all the tribunals created by the new Ecclesiastical Jurisdiction Measure.[4]

From very ancient times the Church has had her own courts; but in England, until the Conquest, both the Shire Court and the Hundred Court exercised jurisdiction in spiritual and in temporal matters alike. William the Conqueror put an end to this in 1072. Thereafter the two jurisdictions were separate. But matters matrimonial, matters testamentary, and defamation were within the ecclesiastical jurisdiction until the middle of the nineteenth century, when, in the great legal reforms of that period, they were removed to the temporal courts.[5] Since then, for all practical purposes, the ecclesiastical courts have confined themselves to matters which are manifestly ecclesiastical. Of recent years, moreover, no attempt has been made to invoke a jurisdiction which has never been abolished over the moral life and orthodoxy of non-ecclesiastical *personae*.[6] For centuries the two main courts of first instance were, in each diocese, the Archdeacon's Court and the Consistory Court, both presided over by trained lawyers. In the nineteenth century the Archdeacon's Court virtually ceased to function. This was

[3.] Halsbury, vol. 14, para. 1268 and *Mackonochie* v. *Lord Penzance*, [1881] 6 App. Cas. 424, H.L.

[4.] 1963, No.1. See pp.143 et seq.

[5.] By the Matrimonial Causes Act, 1857 (20 & 21 Vict., c. 85), the Court of Probate Act, 1857 (20 & 21 Vict., c. 77), and the Ecclesiastical Courts Act, 1855 (18 & 19 Vict., c. 41) respectively.

[6.] 'Non-ecclesiastical *personae*' is a more accurate expression than 'the laity'. Though it seems highly improbable that today anyone would attempt to bring proceedings in an ecclesiastical court against an ordinary layman in respect of his personal opinions or moral behaviour, ecclesiastical *personae* such as chancellors and churchwardens might in some circumstances find themselves the objects of such proceedings.

largely because as a court of first instance its jurisdiction in many matters overlapped with that of the Consistory Court and the suitor had the choice of bringing his cause to either court. Since an appeal lay from the Archdeacon's Court to the Consistory Court, the opportunity was usually taken of going straight to the higher tribunal.

From the Consistory Court an appeal lay in most cases to the Provincial Court. In Canterbury this became known as the Court of the Arches from the fact that it usually sat in the arched crypt of the church of St. Mary le Bow in the City of London, where it still at times sits. Its judge became known as the Dean of the Arches. In the northern province the Provincial Court was known as the Chancery Court of York and its judge as the Auditor. From the Provincial Court, before the Reformation, a further and final appeal lay to Rome. At the Reformation appeals to Rome were abolished[7] and in their place a final appeal lay to the King in Chancery,[8] the jurisdiction being in fact exercised by a Commission of Delegates, so that the tribunal came to be known as the Court of Delegates. In the nineteenth century this appellate jurisdiction was transferred to the Judicial Committee of the Privy Council.[9]

This by no means exhausts the list of the ecclesiastical tribunals which at one time or another functioned in England. Some had disappeared by the nineteenth century,[10] and others disappeared during that century; but in their place new tribunals sprang up,[11] and the twentieth century added to the quota.[12] The reader may be thankful that he is no longer concerned, save as a historian, with this multiplicity of courts, for, under the Ecclesiastical Jurisdiction Measure, 1963,[13] many of them were swept away and new machinery was devised

---

[7] Ecclesiastical Appeals Act, 1532 (24 Hen. VIII, c. 12).

[8] Submission of the Clergy Act, 1533 (25 Hen. VIII, c. 19).

[9] Privy Council Appeals Act, 1832 (2 & 3 Will. IV, c. 92).

[10] e.g. there was the Prerogative Court of Canterbury for probate causes.

[11] The Church Discipline Act, 1840 (3 & 4 Vict., c. 86) and the Public Worship Regulation Act, 1874 (37 & 38 Vict., c. 85); the Clergy Discipline Act, 1892 (55 & 56 Vict., c. 32); and the Benefices Act, 1898 (61 & 62 Vict., c. 48).

[12] See, e.g., the Incumbents (Discipline) Measure, 1947 (No. 1); the Incumbents (Discipline) Measure, 1947 (Amendment) Measure, 1950 (No. 1); the Incumbents (Discipline) and Church Dignitaries (Retirement) Amendment Measure, 1953 (No. 3).

[13] No. 1.

for the administration of justice in matters ecclesiastical, and it is to this Measure alone that one need usually turn today. But the reader's relief will probably be short-lived; for when he turns to this Measure, designed very largely to simplify an outdated and complicated system, he will find, in place of the old system, a new one in many respects so cumbersome and unpractical that it is doubtful whether, in some of its aspects, any attempt will be made to use it more than the one time necessary to convince even its authors of its unserviceability for many of the purposes for which it was designed.[14] It is, however, with this system that for good or for ill we are now concerned. But before turning to it mention must be made of the lawyers who have to operate it.

For a time after the Conquest there was no hard and fast distinction between common law lawyers and ecclesiastical lawyers, and many of the former were clerks. For still longer those who were concerned with that special system of the secular law administered in Chancery and known as equity were clerks, the King's Chancellor being usually a highly placed ecclesiastic, the last of whom was Bishop Williams, who succeeded Bacon in 1621 and who, although himself trained in the common law, was not able to sustain the high intellectual standard set by a succession of lay predecessors. Gradually, however, distinct professions emerged. The secular lawyers (the barrister, serjeants, and judges) received their training, and were to be found, in the Inns of Court and Serjeants' Inn. The ecclesiastical lawyers (advocates and judges) qualified in the civil (or Roman) law at the universities and then practised in Doctors' Commons close to St. Paul's Cathedral. In course of time, just as in the secular courts the client went first to his attorney-at-law or solicitor-in-chancery,[15] who, if necessary, engaged the services of a member of the Bar, so in the ecclesiastical courts the client went first to his proctor, who, if

---

14. The author has been reminded that during the debates on the Measure in the Church Assembly he made many criticisms, some of which were accepted and some rejected. Some of those which were rejected are repeated in this chapter, for they appear to the author to be as valid now as when they were made. Inasmuch as they are matters of opinion, it will be for the reader to judge for himself as to their validity. No doubt, in course of time, experience will provide the answer.

15. Later to become one profession—solicitors.

necessary, engaged the services of one of the doctors. With the reforms of the nineteenth century Doctors' Commons disappeared and with it the distinctive professions of ecclesiastical lawyers. Today any solicitor is entitled to act as proctor in the ecclesiastical courts and any barrister or solicitor has a right of audience there. The result, of course, has been to increase the tendency for the law and practice of the temporal and spiritual courts to approximate closely, and this, in turn, has tended still more to differentiate English canon law from canon law in other parts of Christendom.

The work of the ecclesiastical courts, like those of the temporal courts, may be conveniently divided into civil and criminal work, the civil work, as is usually the case, being less spectacular but more basic.[16] Each must be again divided into those matters which involve points of doctrine, ritual, or ceremonial, called reserved cases, and those which do not, called conduct cases. The civil work of the ecclesiastical courts is known as the faculty jurisdiction, and it is with that that our study of the present system of ecclesiastical courts will begin.

2. THE FACULTY JURISDICTION

As has already been noted,[17] the act of consecration brings the land and everything in it or on it under the jurisdiction of the ordinary, which, except in a few cases, means that they come under the faculty jurisdiction. In addition, so does the unconsecrated curtilage of a consecrated church; so do unconsecrated buildings licensed for worship, if the bishop so directs; and so also do the contents of parochial libraries.[18]

---

16. A crime has been defined as an unlawful act or omission, the sanction for which is punitive, which said sanction is remissible only by the Crown, if remissible at all. The main feature of a crime is that its sanction is punitive. The civil law is basic, in that it is concerned with keeping or restoring the *status quo* —with giving persons what they ought to have. Criminal law does nothing directly to achieve this object. It comes into operation only after the law has been broken, and it deals with the offender hoping thereby that he and others may be less disposed to repeat the offence; but it neither restores the *status quo* nor gives persons their rights.

17. Chapter XI *ante*.

18. Certified by the Charity Commissioners as being within the scope of the Parochial Libraries Act, 1708 (7 Anne, c. 14); s. 4 of the Faculties Jurisdiction Measure, 1964 (No.5). See also *Re St. Mary's Warwick* (1981) Fam. 170.

Thereafter a faculty is required before anything is done to the land, the buildings on it, or their contents. Thus, no alteration may be made to the fabric or decoration of a church or in respect of its ornaments and furnishings, whether permanent or temporary, movable or fixed, without the authority of a faculty. Without such authority new ornaments and furnishings may not be introduced into the church, nor those already there removed (even though they were introduced illegally). In practice an exception is made in respect of trivial matters, such as flowers, footstools, literature, new washers, and electric light bulbs, while the doctrine of necessity[19] can justify, and indeed demand, the immediate carrying out of an urgent repair without further authority. Nor does the faculty jurisdiction extend to the clothing of the ministers, which must be controlled, if controlled at all, by the criminal jurisdiction. But it extends to such things as altars, lecterns, pews, bells, windows, aumbries, bookshelves, tablets, candlesticks, chalices, patens, carpets, lighting and heating, and, indeed, everything of any importance for use or decoration in the church. It extends, too, over the churchyard. The body of a parishioner and of anyone dying in the parish may be buried as of right and without a faculty in a churchyard consecrated for that purpose[20] (but not, without a faculty, in the church), but no tombstone may be erected as of right without a faculty, nor, as of right, may ashes be deposited therein without one.[21] A faculty, moreover, may for good cause confer special privileges which have the effect of limiting the rights of others. Thus, it may reserve a pew in the church to the use of a particular individual and the exclusion of others; or, in the churchyard, it may reserve a grave space to a particular person[22] or for a particular purpose (for example, by the setting aside of an area for the deposition of cremated remains), or it may allow a drain or an underground cable to occupy the land. The jurisdiction

---

19. See p. 70 *ante*.
20. See pp. 97 and 98 *ante*.
21. And ashes should never be deposited in the church itself without a faculty. Canon B38, though it may appear to authorize burial of ashes, in all probability does not represent a change in the law; in strict law a faculty ought to be obtained.
22. Though not now for longer than 100 years; s. 8 of the Faculty Jurisdiction Measure, 1964 (No. 5).

extends *usque ad coelum*, so that an overhead wire for a
telephone or light may not be carried over the land without a
faculty.

This jurisdiction is exercised by the judge of the Consistory
Court of the diocese. In the diocese of Canterbury he is known
as the commissary general. In other dioceses he is known as the
chancellor. It is by this term that he is commonly designated,
though he is in all dioceses also the vicar general of the bishop
in spiritualities, official principal of the Consistory Court (in
which capacity he presides as judge), and second only to the
bishop in the diocese.[23] The chancellor may be a layman or a
cleric;[24] but he must be a lawyer who either holds or has held
high judicial office or is a barrister of at least seven years'
standing. He must also be at least thirty years of age and, if a
layman, a communicant.[25] He is appointed by the bishop by
letters patent;[26] but thereupon he becomes an independent
judge in one of the Queen's courts, deriving his authority not
from the bishop, but from the law, and charged, like all judges,
with hearing and determining impartially causes in which the
bishop or the Crown may have an interest.[27] He is thus not
only independent, like all judges, of the authority appointing
him; but, being in no sense a deputy, he is, like the bishop, an
ordinary, and, of course, no appeal lies from him to the bishop,
but only to the appropriate appellate court.[28] Unless his

---

[23] It is a typically English characteristic to exalt the judiciary. For all practical
purposes the Prime Minister is the most important Minister of the Crown; but the
Lord Chancellor takes precedence of him. So, in a diocese, the suffragan bishop
(if any) is usually the person to whom one looks first in the absence of the diocesan;
but the chancellor, by reason of the antiquity and judicial nature of his office, is
theoretically the second person in the diocese.

[24] Chancellors are frequently chancellors of more than one diocese. Excluding Sodor
and Man, there are forty-three English dioceses, but there are only about eighteen
diocesan chancellors, of whom at present two only are in orders.

[25] S.2 of the Ecclesiastical Jurisdiction Measure, 1963 (No.1). Formerly, in the days
of Doctors' Commons, he was always either a Doctor of Civil Law (Oxford) or a
Doctor of Laws (Cambridge), though Canon 127 required no more than that he
should be 26, learned in the civil and ecclesiastical laws, and at least a Master of
Arts or Bachelor of Law, reasonably well practised in the course thereof, well
affected and zealously bent to religion, touching whose life and manners no evil
example is had.

[26] S. 2 ibid.

[27] *Bishop of Lincoln v. Smith* [1668] 1 Vent, 3; *ex parte Medwin*, [1853] 1 E. and B. 609.

[28] See pp.142 and 143 *post*.

appointment is confirmed by the dean and chapter, or other capitular body of the cathedral church, he vacates his position on the advent of a new bishop. But if, as is almost always the case, his appointment is so confirmed, his appointment continues until he is compelled to retire upon attaining the age of 75 years.[29] Formerly he had even greater security than judges of the Supreme Court, for, whereas they can be removed on an address from both Houses of Parliament, a chancellor could be removed only by an Act of Parliament or a Measure of the Church Assembly.[30] But the Ecclesiastical Jurisdiction Measure[31] has now made provision for his removal if the Upper House of the Convocation of the province in which his diocese lies resolves that he is incapable or unfit to act. The chancellor is the sole judge in faculty cases, but the extent of this faculty jurisdiction is determined by the terms of the patent by which he is appointed[32] and thus varies from diocese to diocese, and in some dioceses the patent reserves to the bishop power to act in certain unspecified circumstances which can be ascertained only by reference to the patent itself.[33] In other matters (for example, in criminal matters) the chancellor's jurisdiction does not depend on his patent, but on statutory enactment, and is thus uniform throughout the dioceses, and the bishop has no jurisdiction except the limited jurisdiction specifically conferred on him by the Measure.[34] The

---

[29] Ecclesiastical Judges and Legal Officers Measure 1976 (No. 2). The Measure does not apply to chancellors holding office on or before April 25, 1976, whose appointments continue to be for life or until resignation.

[30] *Dr. Sutton's Case,* [1627] Litt.22; *Jones v. Bishop of Llandaff,* [1693] Mod. Rep. 27.

[31] S. 2.

[32] S. 46, Ecclesiastical Jurisdiction Measure, 1963 (No. 1).

[33] The Chichester patent in particular reserves wide powers to the bishop; see *R. v. Tristram* (1902), 1 K.B. 816. Bishop Bell availed himself of these powers in circumstances which raised considerable misgivings as to the constitutional propriety of his actions. It is, of course, clear that in many cases, whatever reservations the patent may contain, the bishop could not function judicially by reason of his having an interest in the result of the proceedings, and in many more cases the constitutional propriety of his acting would run counter to the English concept of the separation of powers between the executive and the judiciary, while in most cases, except the simplest, he would be ill-equipped in knowledge and training for the task. Cf. the position of the Crown in this respect, for, although the source of all jurisdiction, the Sovereign never acts in person; see Halsbury, vol. 8 para 943 and *Re St. Mary's Barnes* (1982) 1 All E.R. 456.

[34] See pp. 143 et seq. *post.*

Consistory Court has its officers and registry, the registrar being the chief officer of the court, appointed by the bishop. He is assisted by such clerks as he chooses, one of whom is generally appointed apparitor, the name implying that it is he who causes persons to appear before the court.

In order to appear as a party, whether in person or by legal representatives, it is necessary to have an interest in the proceedings sufficient to provide a *locus standi*. The incumbent, the churchwardens, the Parochial Church Council, the parishioners, those whose names are entered on the electoral roll, and the archdeacon are persons with an interest, and, if the archdeacon be absent or ill or unable or unwilling to act, the bishop may appoint someone else for this purpose in his place, the object being to provide someone to represent the interests of the diocese.[35] Indeed, the archdeacon's position in the Consistory Court is analogous to that of the Attorney-General in proceedings concerning trusts in the Chancery Division, and the court often looks to the archdeacon for the same sort of help which the Attorney-General affords to the Chancery Division. It is through the archdeacon that the bishop should intervene, should he wish to do so, and not in person.[36] But, although all these persons are always deemed to have an interest, the list of interested persons is by no means confined to them. Thus, if the proceedings should concern a monument already in the church or churchyard, the owners of the monument[37] and the relatives of the person commemorated would have an interest. So, of course, would anyone against whom an order was sought. If, therefore, it were sought to recover costs or expenses against the person responsible for work done unlawfully without a faculty which it was now sought to rectify, the persons against whom the order was sought have an interest and should be made parties to the proceedings.[38] It is, too, apprehended that possibly persons who wish to do something to a church (for

[35] Faculty Jurisdiction Measure, 1964 (No. 5).

[36] *Harper v. Forbes and Sisson,* [1859] 5 Jur. N. 8. 275. See *Fagg v. Lee,* L.R. 4 A. and E. 135 and (on appeal) 6 P.C. 38. By reason of the Measure, no one can doubt the archdeacon's interest, as in *Noble* v. *Reast* (1904), P.34, when the archbishop's nominee's *locus standi* was rejected.

[37] See p.105 *ante.*

[38] S. 5, Faculty Jurisdiction Measure, 1964 (No. 5).

example, to put in a monument) may have a sufficient interest to make the application; but it may be that in such cases they do not acquire a *locus standi*, and for this reason such an application is often made on their behalf by persons with an undoubted standing, such as the incumbent, the churchwardens, or the Parochial Church Council. A mere volunteer,[39] however, has no *locus standi*, and thus amenity societies, who are concerned for the preservation of a church cannot themselves become parties to the proceedings and are obliged to seek some parishioner who, financed by them, is willing to become a party.[40] But public bodies such as the County or Borough Council may well have an interest in consecrated ground within their territory, and it is apprehended that the Crown always has an interest, the Queen being Supreme Governor of the Church, and possibly the archbishop would also have an interest.[41]

The procedure for obtaining and opposing the grant of a faculty has been fairly uniform throughout the dioceses, but each Consistory Court has had its own practice as part of its inherent jurisdiction. Uniformity, however, is provided over a wide field by the Faculty Jurisdiction Measure 1964,[42] under which rules[43] have been made by a Rule Committee.

All proceedings are begun by a petition in which the petitioners pray the court for a faculty to do whatever it may be that they want to do. In every diocese there is a statutory body called the Diocesan Advisory Committee, consisting of the archdeacons and of such other persons as the bishop may appoint, chosen in the main for their artistic, musical, antiquarian, engineering, or constructional knowledge.[44] It is the duty of these Committees to advise the chancellor, the parties, and others (for example, those responsible for the

---

39. *Noble v. Reast* (1904), P.34.
40. But see p.141 *post*. This and many other matters concerning the Faculty Jurisdiction are under active review by a Commission of the General Synod, and some changes may well soon occur.
41. See *Re St. James, Bishampton, re St. Edburga's Abberton* (1961), 2 All E.R. 1 (Consistory Court) and again p. 429 and p. 430 (Arches Court).
42. No. 5, s. 14.
43. See the Faculty Jurisdiction Rules 1967, S.I. 1967 No. 1002 as amended by S.I. 1975 No. 135.
44. Ibid., s. 13.

upkeep of unconsecrated buildings licensed for worship) on the technical and aesthetic aspects of proposals affecting churches.[45] The petitioner's proposals at some stage, usually before the filing of a petition, should go to the Committee for advice and comment, and this advice, if not already attached to the petition, will be sought by the chancellor. The petition is lodged in the registry and submitted to the chancellor, who reads it and looks at any plans which accompany it and then usually endorses it with a decree for citation. This directs that the petition shall be advertised by a notice on the door of the church. The chancellor may also decree a special citation to persons who he thinks may be interested, or he may direct that the proposals be advertised in the press. If, however, the chancellor is doubtful about whether the proceedings are in order, he may direct that the application for citation shall be made to him in chambers. In the great majority of cases the petition is unopposed and any difficulties concerning the design have been cleared up by the Advisory Committee. In these cases, unless the chancellor is himself doubtful about the proposals and his doubts have not been met by correspondence between the registry and the petitioners, he will decree that a faculty shall issue for what is sought. Indeed, when the papers were before him for citation, he may have decreed that, in the absence of opposition, the faculty should issue. If, however, someone wishes to oppose the petition, he enters an appearance in writing at the registry and follows it with a written pleading,[46] called an act on petition. This may call forth another pleading from the petitioner, called a reply, and this may be followed by still further pleadings until the points in issue are clearly defined. In these cases, and in cases where the

---

45. They and others (the chancellor, for example) may in turn seek advice from another body set up by the General Synod, known as the Central Council of Diocesan Advisory Committees for the Care of Churches. Cathedrals may seek advice from another (non-statutory) body known as the Cathedrals Advisory Committee.

46. Plea and *pleading* are lawyers' terms and are much misunderstood. A barrister does not plead in court; he appears and argues in court. Pleadings are nearly always written documents, exchanged between the parties before the hearing and designed to set forth the points which are agreed and those which are in issue. One of the few oral pleas is the plea of *guilty* or *not guilty* by which in a criminal case the accused replies to the prosecution's written pleading, the indictment.

chancellor himself is not satisfied, the case eventually comes on before him in open court, where, after hearing witnesses and argument, he give his decision, including the decision regarding costs and expenses.

The Consistory Court has all the powers of the High Court with regard to securing the attendance of witnesses by subpoena and the production and inspection of documents.[47] Any order of the Consistory Court with regard to the payment of costs may be enforced in the County Court.[48] Contempt of a Consistory Court is dealt with by the High Court.

Special rules apply to petitions for faculties to demolish churches in whole or in part.[49] Unless the court is satisfied that it is proposed to build another church on the same site, or unless the court is satisfied that so much of the church as is left standing will be used for the public worship of the Church of England, a faculty may issue only if notice of the proposal has been advertised in the *London Gazette*, the Central Council[50] has been notified, and someone from the Central Council has had an opportunity of giving evidence in open court and the chancellor has also heard any other person whose intervention is other than frivolous or vexatious.[51]

Sometimes work may be carried out on the authority of an archdeacon's certificate[52] instead of under faculty. The object of this alternative procedure is simply to save costs.[53] It applies only in the case of a change in the heating system of a church, or for repairs to a church or its contents or for their redecoration where no substantial change in appearance will be effected thereby. The proposals have to be advertised and no notice of objection received. The archdeacon may then either direct that a petition for a faculty be filed, or himself authorize the work by

47. Ecclesiastical Jurisdiction Measure, 1964 (No. 1), s. 81.
48. Faculty Jurisdiction Measure, 1964 (No. 3), s. 11.
49. Ibid., s. 2.
50. See note 45 on p.140 *ante.*
51. This is the one exception to the rule that mere volunteers may not intervene, and it is for the benefit of amenity societies that the exception has been made. See p. ante, and *Re Christ Church, Croydon* (1983) 1 W.L.R. 830.
52. Faculty Jurisdiction Measure, 1964 (No. 5), s. 12.
53. For this reason it is popular with parishes. It is not so popular with registrars, archdeacons, and chancellors, for it involves just as much work for them as a petition for a faculty and usually the application is far less well prepared.

certificate, provided, in the latter case, that the Advisory Committee approves. An archdeacon's certificate may also issue in any other case by direction of the chancellor, if in his opinion the proposal is unlikely to be controversial and does not justify the expense of a faculty.

If anything requiring the authority of a faculty or archdeacon's certificate has been done without such authority, it must, nevertheless, remain unless a faculty is granted to undo it. If, however, it is wished that whatever has been done should remain, a confirmatory faculty should be sought. In such cases it is common for the chancellor to require a hearing in open court with an explanation of why the work was done without authority. It is also common for a petition to be lodged for the removal of unauthorized work and for this petition to be opposed by those responsible for the work, who in turn lodge a cross-petition for a confirmatory faculty.[54] In such cases, even if the cross-petition succeeds, the court may well order that all the costs be paid by the cross-petitioners.

Those who are dissatisfied with a decision of the Consistory Court have rights of appeal to an appellate tribunal. Formerly the scheme was very simple. An appeal lay to the Provincial Court of Appeal. In the southern province this was the Court of the Arches, presided over by the Dean of the Arches, and in the northern province it was the Chancery Court of York, presided over by the same judge in his capacity as Auditor of that court. From the Provincial Court a further appeal lay to the Judicial Committee of the Privy Council. This simple arrangement, however, has now been vastly complicated by the Ecclesiastical Jurisdiction Measure, 1964.[55] Under that Measure the course which an appeal takes depends on whether or not the point involved is one involving a point of doctrine, ritual, or ceremonial (known as a reserved matter), and it is the duty of the chancellor to give a conclusive certificate as to whether or not such a point is involved.

If no such point is involved, the appeal still goes to the Provincial Court. The Dean of the Arches (or Auditor) still presides over it, and it is now provided[56] that he must be a

---

[54] See *Re St. Mary's, Balham* (1978) 1 All E.R. 993.
[55] No. 1.
[56] S. 2, ibid.

barrister of at least ten years' standing or a person who has held high judicial office, and, if a layman, a communicant.

A further appeal in this type of case from the provincial court still lies to the Judicial Committee of the Privy Council.[57]

If, however, the appeal from the Consistory Court is in a matter involving doctrine, ritual, or ceremonial, it no longer goes to the Court of the Arches or to the Chancery Court of York. It goes instead to a new court called the Court of Ecclesiastical Causes Reserved. This consists of five persons appointed by the Crown, of whom two are to be communicants who hold or have held high judicial office and three are to be diocesan bishops or persons who have been diocesan bishops.

From the Court of Ecclesiastical Causes Reserved a further appeal lies, not to the Judicial Committee, but to a new tribunal called a Commission of Review, consisting of five persons, three of whom shall be communicant Lords of Appeal and two shall be diocesan bishops with seats in the House of Lords.[58]

3. CRIMINAL JURISDICTION

The Ecclesiastical Jurisdiction Measure, 1963,[59] has swept away a number of tribunals and procedures which before existed for the trial of persons accused of ecclesiastical offences. The machinery which has gone was complicated and cumbersome. The machinery which has taken its place is, unfortunately, no less so. It is again necessary to consider the position according to whether the offence charged does or does not involve points of doctrine, ritual, or ceremonial. It is also necessary to consider the position according to whether the accused is a priest or deacon, or whether he is a suffragan bishop or a diocesan bishop or an archbishop, or simply a bishop (for example, a retired bishop).

[57.] Consisting, as heretofore, of Lords of Appeal and others who have held or do hold high judicial office.

[58.] It would seem that any appeal involving even the most trivial and well-settled point of doctrine, ritual, or ceremonial, must go through this astonishingly weighty procedure, involving three Lords of Appeal, two judges of Supreme Court standing, and five diocesan bishops, as well as the chancellor, even though the main point in the appeal concerns some quite different matter.

[59.] No. 1. See also the Incumbents (Vacation of Benefices) Measure 1977 (No. 1) p.42 et seq. *ante* which in cases of pastoral breakdown might perhaps be employed instead of taking strictly disciplinary steps.

It will be convenient to consider first a 'conduct case' (as it has come to be called) against a priest or deacon. A conduct case is any offence against ecclesiastical law other than one in respect of doctrine, ritual, or ceremonial.[60] It includes, but is not limited to, conduct unbecoming the office and work of a clerk in holy orders, and serious, persistent, or continuous neglect of duty; but it is expressly provided that proceedings shall not be taken for unbecoming conduct or neglect of duty in respect of political opinions or activities.[61] There is also a limitations clause provided that proceedings are not to be taken in respect of conduct more than three years before the date of the proposed proceedings.[62]

Proceedings may be instituted against any priest or deacon by anyone authorized by the bishop, and against an incumbent by six persons on the relevant electoral roll, and against a stipendiary curate by his incumbent. Proceedings are begun by laying a complaint before the registrar of the diocese and serving it on the accused. It is then considered by the bishop, who must give the complainant and the accused an opportunity of being interviewed by him privately, after which he may either direct that no further steps be taken in the matter or else refer it to an examiner. In every diocese there must be three examiners, who are to be appointed by the Diocesan Synod and who must be barristers or solicitors whom the chancellor considers to be sufficiently experienced. The examiner's task closely resembles that of a committing magistrate. The complainant lays before him affidavit evidence, as may also the accused; the examiner and opposing party may require the deponents to attend for cross-examination, and failure to comply with this requirement is to result in the affidavit's being disregarded.

---

60. The doing of anything which is forbidden, or the neglect of anything which is enjoined, is an offence. The carrying out, without a faculty, of works requiring a faculty would come under this heading, though such a matter is more likely to be dealt with as a civil matter under the faculty jurisdiction than as a criminal matter. See s. 14(2) of the Ecclesiastical Jurisdiction Measure, 1963 (No. 1).

61. Ibid., s. 14(1). As some think, this proviso reflects the sensitivity or even the over-sensitivity of some clergymen in respect of the freedom of the clerical conscience, regardless of whether or not such freedom is maintained at the expense of their effectiveness as ministers bound in conscience to expound the official teaching of the Church which commissions them.

62. Ibid., s. 14(2) and s. 16; but note the proviso in respect of convictions in the secular courts.

Both complainant and accused may be represented before the examiner by 'a friend or adviser'.[63] After inquiry the examiner decides whether or not there is a case to answer. If he decides that there is no case to answer, 'no further step shall be taken in regard thereto'.[64] If the examiner decides that there is a case to answer, the bishop appoints a fit person to prosecute the accused in the Consistory Court. In the Consistory Court the chancellor is the judge,[65] but are two clerical and two lay assessors to exercise the functions of a jury. They are chosen by lot from a panel of six priests and six communicant laymen approved by the Diocesan Synod.[66] The procedure is as near as possible to that of the Crown court. For a conviction, the assessors must be unanimous. If they do not agree, it rests with the chancellor to direct either a new trial or an acquittal. If they convict, the chancellor decides on and passes the sentence (called a *censure*). There are five possible censures, namely:

1. Deprivation, which involves removal from preferment, and disqualification from holding further preferment without the express consent of a diocesan bishop with the consent of the archbishop and of the bishop of the diocese where the censure was imposed. It also renders the accused liable to be deposed from holy orders (or, in common parlance, unfrocked) at the discretion of the bishop, subject to an appeal on this point to the archbishop.[67]

2. Inhibition, which is disqualification for a specified time from exercising any of the functions of his order.

3. Suspension (which may be passed in addition to inhibition), which disqualifies the accused for a specified

---

63. Ibid., s.24. It is to be noted that, while *legal* representation is not excluded, it is not required.

64. Ibid., s.24(5). It is apprehended that this means that the examiner's decision amounts to an acquittal. This is not so in the case of the dismissal of a charge by a committing magistrate for it is always open to the prosecution to bring the charge again, and, in the case of an indictable offence, only the verdict of a jury renders the matter *res judicata*.

65. But, with the consent of the bishop, he may appoint someone else in his place. This provision was inserted to meet the case of a chancellor with little or no criminal experience. A chancellor who has practised at the common law Bar would feel far more at home in a criminal court than one whose practice had been exclusively in Chancery.

66. Ibid., s. 30 and Second Schedule, Part II.

67. But see p.152 *post* for the preservation of the royal prerogative, and ibid., s.49(3). All deans of Cathedrals are appointed by the Crown.

time from performing the duties of his preferment and from residing in the residence which goes with it or in any house within a specified distance of it, save with the bishop's leave.

4. Monition, which is an order to do or not to do a specified act.

5. Rebuke, which means what it says.

From the decision of the Consistory Court an appeal lies to the Court of the Arches (or to the Chancery Court of York) at the suit of the accused on a question of law or of fact and at the suit of the prosecution on a question of law.[68] But for this purpose the Dean (or Auditor) sits with two clerics appointed by the prolocutor of the Lower House of the relevant province, and two communicant laymen appointed by the Chairman of the House of Laity of the General Synod after consultation with the Lord Chancellor and possessing such judicial experience as the Lord Chancellor thinks appropriate.

In one instance it is possible to avoid the whole of this procedure, for if the accused consents, the bishop may, after consultation with the complainant, summarily dispose of the case by passing upon him any of the possible censures.

Certain convictions and orders of the temporal courts automatically render a priest or deacon subject to ecclesiastical penalties without further trial. They are as follows:

1. A conviction for an offence followed by a sentence of imprisonment.

2. An affiliation order.

3. A decree of divorce or judicial separation on the ground of adultery, unreasonable behaviour, or desertion.[69]

4. A finding of adultery in a matrimonial cause.[70]

5. An order made under Section 2 of the Matrimonial Proceedings (Magistrates' Courts) Act 1960.[71]

6. An order made under Section 27 of the Matrimonial Causes Act 1973[72] for wilfully neglecting to maintain his wife or any child of his family.

[68.] The Measure appears to make no provision in this instance for an appeal against sentence. See s. 7.

[69.] See the Matrimonial Causes Act 1973 (21 & 22 Eliz. II, c. 18) s. 1 and s. 17.

[70.] e.g. as co-respondent.

[71.] Now repealed and replaced by Section 2 of the Domestic Proceedings and Magistrates' Courts Act, 1978 (26 & 27 Eliz. II, c. 22).

[72.] 21 & 22 Eliz. II, c. 18.

In all the above cases the bishop must, without further trial, refer the matter to the archbishop, who has a discretion whether or not to make an order of deprivation (if the accused holds preferment) and to declare the accused disqualified from holding preferment.[73]

If it is desired to bring a charge against a priest or a deacon for an ecclesiastical offence involving a matter of doctrine, ritual, or ceremonial (for example, for departing from the rubrics in the Book of Common Prayer during public worship), the proceedings, as in conduct cases, begin with the laying of a charge by a qualified complainant before the registrar of the diocese. The bishop must then afford to the complainant and to the accused an opportunity of being interviewed in private by him, either separately or together.[74] Thereafter the bishop must decide whether or not to let the case go forward.

If the bishop decides that the case shall proceed, there follow committal proceedings, as in conduct cases, but this time they do not take place before an examiner but before a singularly weighty body, called a committee, consisting of one diocesan bishop (appointed by the archbishop), two members of the Lower House of the appropriate Convocation (appointed by the prolocutor), and two diocesan chancellors (appointed by the Dean of the Arches and Auditor). The procedure is the same as in conduct cases before an examiner. At the end of the proceedings, however, the committee has three choices. It may decide that there is no case to answer and dismiss the case. It may decide that there is a case to answer and send the accused for trial. But if it decides that a *prima facie* case has been made out, but that the offence charged is too trivial to warrant further proceedings, or that there are extenuating circumstances, or (and this is a novel provision in legal proceedings) that further proceedings would not be in the interests of the Church of England, it may, having first considered any representations made by the accused and by the bishop, dismiss the case and report to Convocation that it has done so, together with the ground on which it has acted.

If the accused is sent for trial, it is the duty of the Upper

[73.] Ecclesiastical Jurisdiction (Amendment) Measure 1974 (No. 2).
[74.] Ecclesiastical Jurisdiction Measure 1963 (No.1), s. 39. In s. 23 dealing with conduct cases, the words 'either separately or together' do not appear.

House of the appropriate Convocation to appoint a fit person to promote a complaint.[75]

The court to which the accused is sent for trial is not, as in conduct cases, the Consistory Court. It is the weighty Court of Ecclesiastical Causes Reserved,[76] made all the more weighty by the addition of not less than three nor more than five advisers selected by the Dean of the Arches and Auditor from a panel of 'eminent' theologians and 'eminent' liturgiologists[77] drawn up by the Upper Houses of both Convocations and approved by the Lower Houses.

The trial itself, like that in the Consistory Court in a conduct case, is as near as may be to a trial at the Crown Court, and, if the accused is found guilty, the court passes sentence on him; but, for a first offence of this nature, monition is the maximum sentence which can be passed.

From the decision of the Court of Ecclesiastical Causes Reserved a further apppeal lies to a Commission of Review appointed by the Crown[78] at the suit of either party on a question of law and at the suit of the accused on a question of fact.[79]

It may seem to many that this formidable array of tribunals with its formidable personnel (in all, six diocesan bishops, three Law Lords, two judges of Supreme Court standing, and two chancellors, not to mention the theological assessors and the diocesan bishop who first considered the complaint) provides a very heavy sledgehammer to crack a possibly insignificant nut. The explanation is probably to be found in part in a fear of a repetition of the ritual prosecutions of the nineteenth century and a dislike for the decisions reached on these matters by the Judicial Committee of the Privy Council—decisions based, it is thought, on an inadequate understanding by the secular judges of the history and development of doctrine, ritual and ceremonial. This dislike has been given overt expression in

---

75. Ecclesiastical Jurisdiction Measure, 1963 (No. 1), s. 43. Compare this with s. 25, where, in conduct cases, it is the bishop who must appoint someone to promote the complaint.
76. See p.143 *ante.*
77. Ibid., s.45.
78. See p.143 *ante.*
79. But not apparently on sentence: see s. 11, Ecclesiastical Jurisdiction Measure, 1963 (No.1) and p.146 *ante.*

section 45(3) of the Measure,[80] which states that the Court of Ecclesiastical Causes Reserved shall not be bound by any decision of the Privy Council in relation to matters of doctrine, ritual, or ceremonial. It is thus open to the court to consider afresh points on which the validity of the Judicial committee's decisions is questioned,[81] and a similar provision is made with regard to the Commission of Review; but the Commission is bound by decisions of previous Commissions, unless fresh information or evidence is adduced on the point in question.[82]

While in secular affairs the tendency of the age seems to be towards egalitarianism, with the result that peers have lost their doubtful privilege of trial in the House of Lords and have to be content with trial in an ordinary court, no such levelling influences seem to have affected the Church Assembly, for the Ecclesiastical Jurisdiction Measure, 1963,[83] makes different provision for the trial of bishops from those provisions made for the trial of the inferior clergy (the priests and deacons).

In a conduct case against a bishop, the proceedings are begun by the laying of a complaint before the registrar of the relevant province. The persons who may lay the complaint against a diocesan bishop are anyone authorized to do so by the archbishop, or any ten persons of whom five must be incumbents in the bishop's diocese and five must be lay members of his Diocesan Synod; and those who may lay a complaint against a suffragan bishop are anyone authorized by the archbishop, or the bishop who commissioned the suffragan, or any ten persons of whom five must be incumbents in the same diocese and five must be lay members of that Diocesan Synod, or, if the accused suffragan is also an incumbent, six persons of full age whose names are on the electoral roll of the parish; and those who may lay a complaint against any other bishop (for example, a retired bishop) are the bishop of the diocese where the accused lives or holds preferment, or anyone authorized by the archbishop, or, if the accused is an incumbent, any six persons of full age on the electoral roll of his parish.

---

80. Ibid.
81. That is not to say that this could have been achieved far more effectively by machinery far less cumbersome.
82. S. 48, Ecclesiastical Jurisdiction Measure, 1963 (No. 1).
83. No. 1.

The committal proceedings, which are conducted like other criminal proceedings under the Measure,[84] take place before a committee consisting of the archbishop and two other diocesan bishops, who, since they are no more capable of performing judicial functions than are justices of the peace, must sit with a legal assessor who must be a communicant and a barrister of ten years' standing or someone who has held high judicial office. The committee may dismiss the case, if it thinks there is no case to answer, or, if it thinks that there is a case to answer, it must commit the accused for trial and appoint someone to prosecute.

The tribunal to try a bishop in a conduct case is a commission consisting of the Dean of the Arches and Auditor as president and four diocesan bishops of the same province, other than a complainant or one who was a member of the committing committee,[85] appointed by the Upper House of the appropriate Convocation. The procedure is, so far as possible, to be the same as that of the Crown Court, but the decisions are to be by a majority.[86] The commission, however, does not pass sentence; in the case of a conviction the matter is referred to the Upper House of the appropriate Convocation, which may pronounce any of the possible censures. But, in order to preserve the royal prerogative, no censure of deprivation against anyone holding a Crown appointment (which includes all diocesan and suffragan bishoprics)[87] other than a parochial appointment is to be effective unless confirmed by the Queen in Council.

If either of the two archbishops is charged with a conduct offence, the procedure for other bishops is slightly modified.

If the offence charged relates to his duties as a diocesan, the complaint must be lodged by five incumbents of his diocese and five lay members of his Diocesan Synod. If it relates to his duties as metropolitan, it must be laid by two diocesan bishops of his province.

---

84. See p.144 *ante*.

85. It does not seem to have occurred to the Church Assembly that great difficulty may be experienced in finding seven bishops (three on the committing committee and four on the commission) from the same province as the accused who do not know him so well as to render them scarcely fit to try him.

86. It will be noted that, unlike a conduct case in the Consistory Court, there is no desirable separation of functions between judge and jury, that four of the judges charged with deciding points of law as well as of fact are legally unqualified, and that there can be a conviction by a bare majority-verdict.

87. As well as deaneries and other appointments. See pp.49 and 53 *ante*.

The committal proceedings take place before a committee consisting of the three senior diocesan bishops of his province, sitting with a legal assessor.

The commission to try him consists of the Dean of the Arches and Auditor sitting with four diocesan bishops appointed by a joint meeting of the two Upper Houses of Convocation, and a similar joint meeting decides the censure, if there is a conviction, subject again to confirmation by the Queen in Council in the case of deprivation.

From a commission appointed to try an archbishop or a bishop an appeal lies to a Commission of Review appointed by the Crown.[88]

In the event of there being a finding in a secular court against a bishop such as would, in the case of a priest or deacon, render him liable to censure,[89] it is for the archbishop to make a declaration of deprivation and disqualification unless he determines that in the circumstances no such declaration should be made; and, if it is against an archbishop that the secular court's finding has been made, it is the other archbishop who exercises these powers.[90]

Proceedings against an archbishop or a bishop in respect of a matter of doctrine, ritual, or ceremonial follow much the same course as do such proceedings against a priest or deacon. The possible complainants are the same as in conduct cases and the complaint is laid before the provincial registrar. In the case of a charge against a bishop, the archbishop has the same powers and duties as a diocesan bishop has in such cases against a priest or deacon; but a complaint against an archbishop goes automatically for inquiry by committal proceedings. In both cases the tribunal charged with hearing the committal proceedings is a committee appointed by the Upper House of the appropriate Convocation. One of the persons so appointed must be the Dean of the Arches and Auditor or a deputy nominated by him, being a communicant who holds or has held high judicial office or is a barrister of at least ten years' standing. The others must be of an even number, but the Upper House does not appear to be limited in its choice by the requirement that they shall possess any special qualification.

---

[88] See pp.143 and 149 *ante*.
[89] See pp.140 and 141 *ante*.
[90] S. 56, Ecclesiastical Jurisdiction (Amendment) Measure, 1974 (No. 2).

The committee has the same powers as a committee for the preliminary investigation of a similar charge against a priest or deacon;[91] but, in the case of a charge against an archbishop, the committee's decision must be communicated also to the other archbishop. If the accused is committed for trial, his trial is before the Court of Ecclesiastical Causes Reserved, with the possibility of appeal to a Commission of Review. The possible censures (and the reservation of the royal prerogative) are as before, monition being the gravest censure possible for a first offence.

It remains only to mention a few points common to all legal proceedings.

A free pardon from the Crown operates as effectively in matters ecclesiastical as it does in matters temporal, the Queen being in all causes, ecclesiastical as well as temporal, throughout her dominions supreme. Thus, where 'an archbishop, bishop or other clergyman is deprived or deposed his incapacities shall cease if he receives a free pardon from the Crown, and he shall be restored to any preferment a previously held if it has not in the meantime been filled'.[92]

It should also be noted that deposition from holy orders (or unfrocking) operates as a ban on the performance of clerical functions. It does not operate to remove the indelible character which theologically ordination and consecration are taken to bestow. Anyone, therefore, who has been unfrocked and who later receives a free pardon may exercise his ministry without further ordination, just as one who has relinquished his orders by deed and who later wishes to resume his clerical functions does not require any further ordination. Indeed, in the case of an unfrocked priest (regardless of any question of a free pardon), the Western Catholic view is that any priestly acts done by him are valid, though irregular.

It will be readily appreciated that, while a charge is pending against a clergyman, it may be undesirable for him to exercise his ministry until the conclusion of the case, and it may, indeed, be impossible for him to do so effectively. It is, therefore, provided that a priest or deacon may be inhibited by the bishop *pendente lite*.[93] In such a case, however, the clergyman so

---

91. See p. 147 *ante.*
92. S. 53, Ecclesiastical Jurisdiction Measure, 1963 (No. 1).

inhibited has the right to nominate a fit person to act temporarily in his place. Only if he fails to nominate a person who in the opinion of the bishop is fit can the bishop himself make the necessary provision.

Since some places are extra-diocesan,[94] it has been enacted that, for the purposes of the Measure, such places shall be deemed to be within the diocese which surrounds them or, if surrounded by more than one diocese, within such one of them as the archbishop may direct.[95] But royal peculiars[96] escape the Measure, and so presumably in such cases recourse can be made only to the visitatorial jurisdiction.

In all legal proceedings costs loom large. They fall heavily, not only on private persons, but also on those in official positions whose duty it may be to take legal proceedings. This has now been recognized, and (following the example of the secular courts) provision has now been made whereby both the prosecution and the defence may be assisted out of funds provided in some cases by the Church Commissioners and in other cases by the Church Commissioners jointly with the Central Board of Finance.[97]

No mention has so far been made of the two complicated procedures of *jus patronatus* and *duplex querela*. The first is to determine which of two claimants has the right to present to a living, and the second is to test the right of the bishop to refuse to institute a presentee. The Benefices Act, 1898,[98] made provision for bringing complaints in this respect against the bishop before a special tribunal consisting of a judge of the Supreme Court and one of the archbishops. But the two old actions were not abolished. The Ecclesiastical Jurisdiction Measure, 1963,[99] reserves to the Consistory Court proceedings upon any *jus patronatus* and to the Court of Ecclesiastical Causes Reserved all suits of *duplex querela*.

[93.] Ibid., s. 77. No similar provision appears to have been made in the case of a bishop or archbishop who is charged with an offence, though provision is made by ss. 71 and 72 in the case of all clerics who have actually been censured to inhibition or suspension for the exercise by someone else of their functions during the period of the inhibition or suspension.

[94.] See Chap. V *ante*.

[95.] S. 66, Ecclesiastical Jurisdiction Measure, 1963 (No. 1).

[96.] See p.53 *ante*.

[97.] Ss. 58-63 (inclusive), Ecclesiastical Jurisdiction Measure, 1963 (No. 1).

[98.] 61 & 62 Vict., c. 48.

[99.] No. 1, ss. 6 and 10.

XV

DISPENSATION

Since human foresight is limited, there is no system of manmade law which forsees and provides for every contingency. The divine law no doubt does do so. But the divine law is apprehended and interpreted by fallible humans (pace Rome). Canon law is no exception. It follows, therefore, that the law of the Church, like the law of the State, fails at times adequately to meet a situation which was never envisaged at the time that any particular law was formulated. This is especially apparent where the law is enshrined in a deliberate enactment, as is the case of an Act of Parliament, for this type of law does not admit of elasticity in interpretation. As with Pilate, what Parliament has written, it has written, and so the law remains, for good or for ill, until Parliament sees fit to pass amending or repealing legislation. Meanwhile unforeseen and exceptional cases from time to time arise and hardship results. Case-law, such as English common law, suffers less from this defect, for it is gradually built up by a series of judicial decisions over the be modification in its expositions as fresh situations arise. But, even so, there is always a tendency for what was fluid to solidify and become rigid. This is exactly what happened to the common law in the Middle Ages. The common law judges became set in their ways, and in their hands the common law eventually failed to develop so as to meet the needs of a changing society. The situation today would be met by legislation, though it is to be noted that in this respect legislation seldom anticipates hardship, but rather, hardship having already occurred, its repetition is obviated by legislation. In the Middle Ages the situation was not met by legislation, for in those days legislation was blessedly rare. It was met instead by the development of that supplementary system of law, administered by the King's Chancellor, which we now call equity. This, in its turn, in time grew rigid, until it, together with the common law, received a new lease of life by the marriage of the two brought about by the Judicature Acts of 1873 and 1875.

This failure of the law to meet exceptional cases has, in the case of temporal law, been met in a variety of ways, the most obvious of which has been the exercise of some dispensing power. But a dispensing power has its dangers. When exercised by the supreme legislative authority, it can lead to an arbitrary absolutism; and, when exercised by some other person or body, it can lead to an autocracy which soon claims to be above the law. The Stuarts claimed to possess this dispensing power, and this claim played no small part in the downfall of James II. Possibly this claim, like other Stuart claims, was justified in law. The Stuarts lost their struggles on the field of battle, and, because they irrevocably lost, there is a tendency to regard their causes as bad. This, however, by no means follows. At a time when our modern Constitution was being hammered out, it was sometimes difficult to say where in law the right lay. It does not follow that the side which ultimately prevailed in war was the side with the better claim in law. But, be that as it may, the royal claim to possess the power of dispensation was too closely allied to a claim that the supreme legislative authority resided in the king in person rather than in the King in Parliament, and on both counts Parliament won. The royal claim to possess a power of dispensation went for ever with James II, at least in the form in which the claim was made. It was a claim to dispense from the provisions of the law both before an act was done and after it was done. In the first case, what would otherwise have been an unlawful act became, by virtue of the dispensation, one which could lawfully be done. In the second case, a person who performed an unlawful act was, by virtue of the dispensation, freed from the consequences of his illegality.

Both forms of royal dispensation disappeared. But something was needed to take their place. Fortunately other alternatives were to hand.

To a limited extent, the doctrine of necessity[1] could operate to mitigate the rigidity of the law. But its operation has always been a little uncertain. For this reason an Act of Indemnity with retrospective effect has its attractions and has occasionally been employed. It has never been doubted that the supreme legislative authority can dispense with the effect of any laws which owe their existence, directly or indirectly, to the will of

[1] See p.70 *ante.*

that authority. No one, therefore, can question the dispensing efficacy of an Act of Parliament. The royal prerogative of pardon survived the fall of James II, and, like the Act of Indemnity, the effect is to relieve a person from the consequences of his unlawful acts. It is, however, more limited in its scope, for, whereas an Act of Indemnity relieves a person of all the consequences of his illegal act, civil and criminal, a pardon does no more than relieve him of his criminal liability, leaving him vulnerable to any civil claims which may have accrued. Its use, furthermore, has in practice tended to be confined to those cases where it subsequently becomes clear that there has been a miscarriage of justice resulting in a wrongful conviction. Though the expression 'pardon' seems singularly inappropriate to cases where it is shown that nothing has occurred to require forgiveness, that in practice is the main use to which this exercise of the royal prerogative has been put.

Both a free pardon and an Act of Indemnity are retrospective in their operation. With the disappearance of the dispensing power of the king, secular law in England has been left with nothing which can in advance legalize an otherwise illegal act. All that is left is an Act of Parliament which does not so much dispense from the law as actually alter the law.

The same problem as faces the State also faces the Church. The need occasionally to dispense from canon law arises. Indeed, in one respect the Church's position is more difficult than that of the State; for in a secular State one can usually find the sovereign power which can make and unmake laws at will and which can, accordingly, if so disposed, legislate for particular cases. In England, therefore, the Queen in Parliament can meet any situation by legislation. But the Church's authority is no more than a delegated authority[2] and her legislative powers are those of subordinate legislature. If she acts contrary to the divine law, her actions are *ultra vires*, and this is so whether she acts by way of legislation or by way of dispensation. Her dispensing powers, therefore, are limited to matters within the scope of her delegated authority. Clearly there can be no complaint on this score, provided that the divine law has been correctly ascertained and accurately formulated.

[2.] See Chapter I *ante*.

This is and always has been the view of Orthodoxy. In the East the need for a dispensing power was recognized quite early and went by the name of economy,[3] as pertaining to the management of a household, in this case the household of God. God himself employed something akin to economy when, by the Incarnation, he set in train a process whereby Man's salvation might be attained despite the consequences of sin which would otherwise inevitably lead to damnation. Taking the Incarnation as her example, the Orthodox Church has regarded the prime purpose of economy to be for the salvation of souls, and, therefore, considers that it should be used when some departure from a rule is more likely to work towards salvation than would an insistence on the rule. Thus, there are occasions when it is better to celebrate the Liturgy at an unauthorized time or in an unauthorized place rather than not to celebrate the Liturgy at all. It is by the application of the principles of economy that, in such circumstances, despite the regulations, the Liturgy may be celebrated.

We need not here deal with the somewhat elusive rules evolved in the East concerning the authorities who may exercise economy and the circumstances in which they may do so. It would seem to be a tenet of Orthodoxy that no economy can be employed to vary the divine law, though, over the matter of divorce, the Orthodox Church comes periliously near this, the argument apparantly being that, though God has joined together two persons so that man may not put them asunder, the Church, as representing God, may do so. In the West, under the legalistic influence of Rome, dispensation[4] has developed with far greater detail and precision. At first it was thought that it could operate only for the good of the Church as a whole, but later it was extended for the benefit of individuals. It was thought that legislative authority and authority to dispense went together, so that a bishop or a synod had power to dispense from his or its own laws, but not from those that were received from above. But a superior legislative authority could dispense from the laws of a suboridnate authority. The

---

3. Oikonomia.

4. Dispensatio, or stewardship, and, therefore, much the same as oikonomia, or the management of a household.

pope, claiming supreme legislative power, claimed also the supreme dispensing power, and gradually the idea developed that all dispensing power derived from the pope and was exercised either by him, or, if by some subordinate authority, only as a power delegated to it by the pope. Not only did the number of cases increase in which dispensations were granted solely for the benefit of individuals instead of for the benefit of the Church, but there was also a significant increase in the actual authority claimed. Originally, in strict compliance with the theory that the Church's authority to legislate is only a delegated authority, subordinate to the divine law, popes gradually began tacitly to assume authority to dispense from the divine law itself. The claim was not so much expressly made as implicitly made by purported acts of dispensation. It was the largeness of these claims and the suspicion that dispensations were granted to individuals solely for their own benefit and in return for payment which in some degree led to the Reformation and to a half-hearted attempt by the Council of Trent to deal with abuses.

This was the rather confused heritage with which in this respect England found herself saddled at the Reformation. To English minds it was clear that the papal claim, explicit or implicit, to dispense from the divine law was excessive. In any event the papal claim to dispense at all in England was repudiated. But the need for a dispensing power was realized. How was it to be found and what was it to be? The answer to this, as to every other problem, could now be supplied only by Act of Parliament. Accordingly, the Ecclesiastical Licences Act, 1533,[5] was passed. It forbade the king's subjects, and even the king himself, from making suit to Rome for a dispensation, and it purported to bestow upon the Archbishop of Canterbury authority to grant such dispensations as formerly might have been obtained from Rome, subject in unusual cases to the royal assent, but not for any cause or matter repugnant to Scripture or the law of God. It also purported to preserve to all bishops such dispensing powers as were accorded to them by the common law or the custom of the realm.

The effect of this piece of legislation is by no means clear,

[5.] 25 Hen. VIII, c.21.

especially since much of the little dispensing which occurs today is regulated by later legislation. The Prayer Book (Alternative and Other Services) Measure, 1965[6] is an example of a later enactment which bestows a dispensing power on various subordinate authorities to authorize departures from the Book of Common Prayer.

In 1621 George Abbot, Archbishop of Canterbury, had the misfortune while hunting accidentally to kill a gamekeeper. It was then thought that by canon law this automatically suspended him from all ecclesiastical functions, and both Williams and Laud, then awaiting consecration as bishops, felt so strongly on the point that they refused consecration at Abbot's hands. The question was how to grant Abbot the dispensation which would enable him once again to function as archbishop. In the end, and after much inquiry and argument, James I (who thought the whole matter ridiculous) executed a curious document which both purported to dispense Abbot and also empowered a commission of bishops to dispense him, which the commission duly did. The incident shows the confusion of thought which existed after the Reformation with regard to dispensation. The course which was followed has in it an element of royal claim to dispense together with an element of recognition of the episcopal power preserved by the Ecclesiastical Licences Act, 1533.[7]

Until recently the most obvious exercise by the Archbishop of Canterbury of the dispensing power was in granting a dispensation for the ordination of anyone born out of wedlock, bastardy providing a canonical bar to ordination (unless dispensed) until the passing of The Clergy (Ordination and Miscellaneous Provisions) Measure, 1964.[8] The issue of the Archbishop's special marriage licence is another example, while the issue by the diocesan chancellor by delegation from the bishop of a common marriage licence, dispensing with the neccessity for banns, is an example of the power preserved to bishops by the Ecclesiastical Licences Act, 1533.[9]

[6.] No. 1, now repealed. The relevant powers are now contained in Canons B2, B4, B5, and B5A. See p.66 et seq. *ante.*
[7.] 25 Hen. VIII, c.21.
[8.] No. 6. See now Canon C2 and C4.
[9.] 25 Hen. VIII, c.21.

If the grant of a free pardon be an exercise of the dispensing power (as it would seem to be), the royal prerogative in this aspect is expressly reserved in ecclesiastical matters by the Ecclesiastical Jurisdiction Measure, 1963.[10] But, as has been indicated, this can operate only retrospectively and only so as to avoid the penal consequences in a criminal matter.

Two questions remain.

The first is as to whether the dispensing power in the Church of England is, for most practical purposes, as dead as is generally thought, or whether a closer study of the Ecclesiastical Licences Act, 1533,[11] together with the state of the canon law in England on this point immediately prior to the Reformation, may reveal a considerably wider power than in practice at least is generally recognized to exist.

The second question is as to how far, if at all, a dispensing power is desirable, and, if desirable, the person or persons in whom it should be vested. Its suspected abuse by Rome was a contributing factor towards bringing about the Reformation. The use to which, in secular matters, it was put by the first four Stuarts helped to bring about the Revolution of 1688. It is certainly capable of being a dangerous power. But the question still remains as to whether it is one which can with convenience be discarded to the extent which in practice has occurred.[12]

---

10. No. 1, ss. 53 and 83 (2) (a).
11. 25 Hen. VIII, c.21.
12. For further reading, see *Dispensation in Practice and Theory*, being the Report of a Commission appointed by the Archbishop of Canterbury in 1935 (SPCK 1944): also *Royal Supremacy and the Trials of Bishops 1558-1725*, by R.E. Head (SPCK 1962): also an article by the author on 'Dispensation' in the *Encylopaedia Britannica*.

XVI

OTHER RELIGIOUS BODIES

The Church of England is that branch of the Catholic Church established in England. As such she claims to be the Catholic Church in this land and, if pressed, she will make this claim to the exclusion of the claims of any other religious body. Her relations with other religious bodies are happily increasingly close and friendly, and, where charity prevails, it is often inappropriate to emphasize claims. But in a book about the law it is impossible to avoid the mention of them. Thus, while the Church and the law alike acknowledge the right of the individual to pursue the beliefs and practices which his conscience dictates, the Church of England claims that within this realm hers is the one authentic jurisdiction. She may be fallible, for, as other Churches have erred,[1] so presumably may the Church of England; but to her is entrusted the power and the authority,[2] and neither the Bishop of Rome[3] nor the Methodist Conference nor any other person or body has any jurisdiction here save that which individuals voluntary choose to accord, nor, ideally, should other ministries be exercised, save by arrangement with the Church of the land. What the Church of England claims for herself in England she accords to others elsewhere.[4] The Bishop of Rome *has* jurisdiction in Rome, and the Orthodox Patriarch of Jerusalem has jurisdiction in Jerusalem, and the Church of England is diffident about trespassing in the sphere which she admits another Church can rightly claim. Thus the Church of England was careful to call her episcopal representative in Jerusalem the Archbishop *in* Jerusalem and not the Archbishop *of* Jerusalem,[5] and he in turn is careful to work there only in accordance with an understanding reached with the Orthodox Patriarch. On this principle, in the nineteenth century the

---

1.   Thirty-nine Articles, Article XIX.   2.   Ibid., Articles XX and XXXIV.
3.   Ibid., Article XXXVII.   4.   Ibid., Article XXXIV.
5.   Now the Bishop in Jerusalem.

Lambeth Conference hesitated to approve a proposal that Anglican bishops should consecrate a bishop for the small Protestant Episcopal communities in Spain and Portugal. Eventually this was done, in the teeth of considerable Anglican opposition, by three bishops of the Church of Ireland, but only on condition that it was made clear that the person consecrated limited his claims to jurisdiction to the Protestant Episcopalians, and made no claim inconsistent with the territorial claims of the Roman hierarchy.[6] In places where another Church is functioning as the authentic Church of that territory, the Church of England on the whole seeks to confine her ministrations to the care of British nationals. But the unhappy divisions into which Christendom has split have rendered inevitable many anomalies. An autonomous Church overseas (in Portugal, for example) may not be prepared to minister to a member of the Church of England, and doctrinal differences between the Churches may, if considerable, result in a considerable modification of the attitude which the Church of England would like to adopt. Thus, the fact that the Established Kirk of Scotland is Prebyterian makes it inevitable that full provision should be made outside the Kirk for the spiritual needs of that minority which, to Anglican eyes, professes the full Catholic faith, namely, the Episcopalians; and in this instance the obvious way to effect this is to acknowledge fully the unestablished Scottish Episcopal Church, whose doctrines are identical with those of the Church of England, but whose genesis was independent of England. When the folly and wickedness of man has broken the unity of Christ's undivided Church into a thousand pieces, it is not surprising that the resulting situation should be confused, as, indeed, it is. In consequence, the law too as it affects the Church of England is also confused and confusing, and only a description of the law in barest outline will be attempted here.[7]

6. The Archbishop of Canterbury was also influenced by the consideration that bishops of an Established Church should be more circumspect than bishops of an unestablished Church about intervening in the affairs of another country. See Archbishop Plunket, by F.D. How, chapters xiv to xix inclusive. See also *The Faith and Order of the Lusitanian and Spanish Reformed Episcopal Churches*, being the Report of a Commission appointed by the Archbishop of Canterbury (1963).

7. See Halsbury (4th ed.), vol. 14, para 313 et seq.

The Church of England is but part, albeit the most influential part, of the world-wide Anglican Communion, which is a body of Churches in full communion with the See of Canterbury and with a common doctrine. Most of these Churches have sprung from the Church of England and some of them are still in some degree dependent on her, while others are wholly autonomous.

The nearest of these Churches (in every respect) is the Church in Wales, for it was part of the Church of England until it was separated and disestablished on 31 March 1920 by virtue of the Welsh Church Act, 1914.[8] Since March 1920 the constitution and government of this disestablished Church have been in accordance with the decisions of that Church itself, reached in pursuance of the provisions for its self-government contained in the Act.

When we turn overseas, we find that the Crown claims supremacy in all matters ecclesiastical as well as temporal throughout the Crown's dominions,[9] but in practice this claim is not pressed, and, since English ecclesiastical law, unlike the common law, does not extend to the Crown's overseas dominions or possessions,[10] the Anglican Churches in the different countries of the Commonwealth are not established Churches, but are voluntary associations on a contractual basis, most of them wholly autonomous, and each governed by its own constitution, which, while not, as in England, part of the law of the land, is nevertheless enforceable contractually and is a branch of the common law.

But, in addition to the autonomous Churches of the Anglican Communion within the Commonwealth and elsewhere (for example, in the United States and in Japan), there are Anglican communities with churches throughout the world for which the Church of England still takes responsibility. Some of these are solely for the benefit of members of the Church of England who happen to be permanently or temporarily in those parts, and examples of these are to be found in northern Europe. Others are partly for such expatriates and partly for missionary

---

[8.] 4 & 5 Geo. V, c.91, read in conjunction with the Welsh Church (Temporalities) Act, 1919 (9 & 10 Geo. V, c.65).
[9.] Thirty-nine Articles, Article XXXVII.
[10.] *Re Lord Bishop of Natal* (1865), 3 Moo, P.C. N.S. 115.

purposes, and the former diocese of Gibraltar provided an example of this type of mixed activity.[11]

The legal relationship of these various bodies to the Church of England varies. The autonomous Churches, wherever they be, scarcely affect the law of England any longer, for those Churches appoint their own bishops, priests, and deacons and are governed each according to its own constitution. Their ministers are, of course, fully recognized by the Church of England. But they are not wholly free to practise their ministry in England. The presentation to a benefice or other preferment in England of a person ordained in the Scottish Episcopal Church may be rejected by the bishop in England at his complete discretion.[12] A person so ordained may officiate in an Anglican church or chapel if he is invited to do so by the incumbent, but he is subject to the same restrictions as an Anglican clergyman in such circumstances.[13] Anyone ordained in England for service overseas or who has been ordained by any bishop other than a bishop of the Church of England or the Church of Ireland or the Church in Wales comes under the Overseas and Other Clergy (Ministry and Ordination) Measure 1967.[14] He requires the permission of the archbishop before he officiates in England; such permission may be limited or unlimited in duration, but so long as it lasts he is in the same legal position as a priest (or deacon) ordained in England. If he is admitted to a benefice the bishop may dispense with the oath of allegiance.

The Royal Supremacy is such that it would seem that no one may here be consecrated a bishop without the royal authority, even though he is to exercise his office abroad. Under licence from the Crown, however, either of the archbishops, with the assistance of other bishops, may in this country consecrate a person to be a bishop overseas.[15] There is, however, presumably, no bar to a consecration without the royal assent,

---

[11.] The Diocese in Europe Measure 1980, (No.2) makes provision for a diocese incorporating the diocese of Gibraltar and the areas of Northern and Central Europe within the jurisdiction of the Bishop of London.

[12.] Episcopal Church (Scotland) Act, 1864 (27 & 28 Vict., c.94).

[13.] Episcopal Church (Scotland) Act, 1964 (12 & 13 Eliz. II. c.12); Canons C8 and C12.

[14.] No. 3

[15.] Bishops in Foreign Countries Act, 1841 (5 Vict., c.6).

provided that the consecration takes place outside the Queen's realms.

Any diocesan bishop in the province of Canterbury or York may at the request of an overseas diocesan bishop ordain the person named in the request, with a view to his exercising his ministry in that overseas diocese.[16] There is power to dispense with the oath of allegiance. The person ordained becomes eligible to exercise his ministry in this country for a limited period providing he is given temporary permission by the archbishop.

By an Order in Council of Charles I congregations abroad of members of the Church of England, if not under the jurisdiction of any other bishop, are under the jurisdiction of the Bishop of London.

The Lambeth Conference, summoned by the Archbishop of Canterbury from time to time, provides a forum for bishops, British or foreign, from the whole of the Anglican Communion. It has no legal status; but its decisions naturally carry great weight in matters of faith and morals. In 1888 it published the statement known as the Lambeth Quadrilateral which sets forth what the Anglican Communion regards as the basis upon which Christendom might be reunited. The four points are as follows: (1) The acceptance of the Old and New Testaments as containing all things necessary to salvation and as the rule and ultimate standard of faith; (2) The Apostles' Creed as the baptismal symbol, and the Nicene Creed as the sufficient statement of the Christian faith; (3) The two dominical sacraments of baptism and the Lord's Supper, with the unfailing use of Christ's words of Institution and of the elements ordained by him; and (4) The historic episcopate, locally adapted in methods of administration to the varying needs of nations and peoples called of God into the unity of his Church. In their dealings with other Christian bodies with a view to reunion the Churches of the Anglican Communion have had the Lambeth Quadrilateral very much to the forefront of their minds.

In this country, although the Church of England is the Established Church, there is virtually complete religious

16. Overseas and other Clergy (Ministry and Ordination) Measure 1967, (No.3) s.5.

freedom, and persons are free to practise their own religion, Christian or non-Christian, or to refrain from practising any religion, entirely as they please, provided, of course, that their practises do not incidentally break the law in some other respect.[17]

There are, however, some circumstances in which the law takes it upon itself to protect religion. It is said to be a common law misdemeanour to blaspheme by denying the existence of God, or to reproach our Lord, or to vilify or ridicule Christianity or the Bible or the Book of Common Prayer.[18] Various specific statutory offences[19] directed against irreverence in one form or another have now been abolished; so blasphemy is now strictly a common law offence.

Religious toleration has had a slow and chequered growth and the marks of old disputes are still visible.[20] For obvious reasons discrimination has been most marked against Roman Catholics, and some traces still remain. Not surprisingly, having regard to the Royal Supremacy and the real part played by the Crown in the affairs of the Church, neither the Sovereign nor the Sovereign's Consort may be in communion with Rome.[21] A Roman Catholic, however, may be Prime Minister; but it is an offence for a Roman Catholic to advise the Crown as to an appointment to any office or preferment in the Church of England,[22] which means that, if a Roman Catholic were to become Prime Minister, some other Minister of the Crown would have to advise on the exercise of the Crown's ecclesiastical patronage, including the appointment to bishoprics. The Lord Chancellor may now be a Roman Catholic, but provision has to be made by Her Majesty in Council for the exercise of his functions (such as visitation and patronage) in relation to the Church of England.[23] Most offices

17. It is, for example, no defence to a charge of manslaughter by neglect for parents to allege that it was contrary to their religious beliefs to summon medical aid for their children: see *R v. Senior* (1899), 1 Q.B. 283.

18. Russell on *Crime* (11th ed.) 1957: and see *R v. Lemon* (1979) 1 All E.R. 898.

19. Sacrament Act, 1547 (1 Edw. VI, c.1), Act of Uniformity, 1558 (1 Eliz. I, c.2) and Act of Uniformity, 1662 (14 Car. Ii, c.4), and Blasphemy Act, 1697 (9 Will. III, c.35).

20. Much that appears in Chapter VI, *ante* is for convenience repeated here.

21. Act of Settlement, 1700 (12 & 13 Will. III, c.2).

22. Roman Catholic Relief Act, 1829 (10 Geo. IV, c.7).

23. Lord Chancellor (Tenure of Office and Discharge of Ecclesiastical Functions) Act, 1974 (22 & 23 Eliz. II, c.25).

in the Church of England are barred to Roman Catholics, nor may a Roman Catholic exercise patronage. If he is the patron of a living, the patronage is exercised by either the University of Oxford or the University of Cambridge; and, if the patronage is his by virtue of his holding some office under the Crown, it is exercised by the Archbishop of Canterbury.[24] A Roman Catholic, however, may be appointed a churchwarden; but, if a priest, he might, even before the Churchwardens (Appointment and Resignation) Measure, 1964,[25] decline to serve, and, if not a priest, he might appoint a deputy.[26] It is an offence for anyone, Roman Catholic or otherwise (and, of course, it was against Roman Catholics that the legislation was aimed), to assume without authority the title of any bishopric or deanery already appropriated to the Church of England.[27]

So far as members of other religious bodies (and persons of no religion) are concerned, there are, for all practical purposes no disabilities at all.

More important than the disabilities (actual or theoretical) attaching to persons who are not members of the Established Church are the provisions made for their benefit.

Their ministers (including Roman Catholic priests) are exempted from jury service,[28] and, like clergymen of the Establishment, are specially protected while conducting religious services,[29] and Dissenting ministers are exempt from service as churchwardens.[30] All Protestant Nonconformists who chose to make the required declaration were exempt from any penalties (now abolished) to which they might otherwise theoretically have been liable for failing to attend divine worship in a church of the Establishment.[31] The places of

---

[24.] Roman Catholic Relief Act, 1791 (31 Geo. III, c.32) and Toleration Act, 1688 (1 Will. & Mar., c.18).

[25.] No. 3

[26.] Ibid.

[27.] Roman Catholic Relief Act, 1829 (10 Geo. IV, c.7) and Ecclesiastical Titles Act, 1871 (34 & 35 Vict., c.53).

[28.] Toleration Act, 1688 (1 Will. & Mar., c.18); Roman Catholic Relief Act, 1791 (31 Geo. III, c.32); Nonconformist Relief Act, 1799 (19 Geo. III, c.44); and Juries Act, 1974 (22 & 23 Eliz. II, c.23).

[29.] Offences against the Person Act, 1861 (24 & 25 Vict., c.100).

[30.] Toleration Act, 1688 (1 Will. & Mar., c.18) and Nonconformist Relief Act, 1779 (19 Geo. III, c.44).

[31.] Toleration Act, 1688 (1 Will. & Mar., c.18); Religious Disabilities Act, 1846 (9 & 10 Vict., c.59); both now repealed.

worship of any religious body may be registered, and, as a result, they obtain relief in respect of rates and may be licensed for marriages.[32] Statutory provision has been made for the inter-denominational sharing of church buildings by means of sharing agreements entered into by the appropriate authorities within the Churches concerned.[33] Marriages may be solemnized according to the forms and ceremonies of any religious body, provided the appropriate words, where laid down by statute, are said and that there is compliance with other minimal conditions.[34] The Education Act, 1944,[35] goes out of its way to respect the religious scruples of parents. Though the schoolday in county and voluntary schools is to begin with collective worship, such worship is not to 'be distinctive of any religious denomination' (however it is thought that this can be achieved) and the religious instruction is to be in accordance with a syllabus agreed by the various denominations, containing no formulary or catechism distinctive of any religious denomination (which would seem that, while it may be instructive, it is not so likely to be educational). But, even so, it lies with the parents to decide whether or not their children are to attend the worship or the religious instruction, and, if possible, facilities are to be afforded for the attendance of the child elsewhere for worship or religious instruction, if the parents so desire.

In law the basic position of religious bodies outside the Establishment is the same as that of any other body which exists for any other purpose. The basis is contractual and depends upon the agreement of the members. The only exception to this general principle arises when Parliament chooses to intervene by legislation. Just as Parliament has seen fit to legislate for Friendly Societies and Trade Unions, so it has at times legislated for religious bodies. Examples of such legislation are to be found in the disabilities and reliefs just mentioned. A more fundamental example is the Methodist Church Union Act,

---

32. Places of Worship Registration Act, 1855 (18 & 19 Vict., c.81); Liberty of Religious Worship Act, 1855 (18 & 19 Vict., c.86); Marriage Act, 1949 (12, 13, & 14 Geo. VI, c.76). In the cases of Quakers and Jews registration is not required.
33. Sharing of Church Buildings Act, 1969 (17 & 18 Eliz. II, c.38) and Sharing of Church Buildings Measure, 1970 (No.2).
34. Marriage Act, 1949 (12, 13, & 14, Geo. VI, c.76)
35. 7 & 8 Geo. VI, c.31.

1929,[36] which was passed to facilitate the union of several branches of Methodism. Once passed, such legislation, of course, binds the Methodists and everyone else until repealed, and to that extent it limits the freedom of action of the members. Even more radical is the legislation which is passed in order to disestablish a Church or a part of a Church, as in the cases of the Church of Ireland and the Church in Wales.[37] Such legislation necessarily provides the framework within which the members of the disestablished body are to operate, and, although great freedom may be bestowed upon the members to enable them to manage their own affairs and to change their constitution, the members nevertheless remain confined to that framework, which can be modified only by further legislation.

It has become customary to drop the old appellations, Nonconformist and Dissenting, and instead to speak of those Protestant bodies in England which are not part of the Establishment as the Free Churches. It is a description which the members of those bodies have chosen for themselves. It is, however, not a very accurate description. This chapter has sought to demonstrate what was said in the first two chapters, namely, that no person and no body can escape the secular power, be that power prince or Parliament or anything else which is sovereign. The secular power, if it wishes, can in law control non-established bodies, and, if it wishes, it can leave established bodies to their own devices. In this context establishment, non-establishment, and disestablishment are immaterial. What does matter is the extent to which the secular power wishes to interfere. That is the pertinent consideration when the disestablishment of the Church of England is being mooted. How much control will the State exercise over a disestablished Church? How much freedom will the State extend to a Church which remains established?

Whatever the Church and wherever the State, the hard, inescapable fact remains that in the ultimate resort the Sovereign Power is and must always be over all persons and in all causes, as well ecclesiastical as temporal, throughout its dominions supreme.

---

36. 19 & 20 Geo. V, c.lix.
37. Irish Church Act, 1869 (32 & 33 Vict., c.42) and Welsh Church Act, 1914 (4 & 5 Geo. V, c.91).

INDEX